POETRY now

THE WORLD VERSUS HUMANS

Edited by

Heather Killingray

First published in Great Britain in 1999 by
POETRY NOW
1-2 Wainman Road, Woodston,
Peterborough, PE2 7BU
Telephone (01733) 230746
Fax (01733) 230751

HB ISBN 0 75430 586 4
SB ISBN 0 75430 587 2

FOREWORD

Although we are a nation of poetry writers we are accused of not reading poetry and not buying poetry books: after many years of listening to the incessant gripes of poetry publishers, I can only assume that the books they publish, in general, are books that most people do not want to read.

Poetry should not be obscure, introverted, and as cryptic as a crossword puzzle: it is the poet's duty to reach out and embrace the world.

The world owes the poet nothing and we should not be expected to dig and delve into a rambling discourse searching for some inner meaning.

The reason we write poetry (and almost all of us do) is because we want to communicate: an ideal; an idea; or a specific feeling. Poetry is as essential in communication, as a letter; a radio; a telephone, and the main criteria for selecting the poems in this anthology is very simple: they communicate.

Contents

Look

Look.
Can you see the acid
in the rain?
No.

Look.
Can you see the forest
killed in vain?
No.

Look.
Can you see the tears
in children's eyes?
No.

Look.
Can you see the sea
without its life?
No.

Look.
Can you see the sky
with all its holes?
No.

Look.
Can you see the tigers
die for their bones?
No.

Look. Please!

Caz Fisher

Paper Plea

These past few years, in many jobs,
The paperwork has grown
Like cells within an infant's brain.
It's multiplied. I hone
Each missive as it hits my desk,
Its bottom I extract
To write down lists or messages.
I also use the back.
The wastage is incredible.
My files can hold no more.
I wish they'd use less paper,
I can hardly reach my door.
To throw it, unrecycled,
Seems a crime, a waste of trees.
I beg you all in management,
Think green, think 'less' - think, please!

Moira Vaughan

Golden Lion Tamarin

I see you peeping through the leaves
Your ruff aflame,
Sweet golden lion Tamarin.

I see you playing in the boughs
Your bright eyes shining.
I hear your happy chatter.

I see you clutch your baby
To your breast,
Innocent of man's desire
To deforest and pollute.

I see you turn bewildered
Eyes and trembling body
To the Brazilian sky,
Lit up by forest fire.

Margaret Carl Hibbs

STOP AND THINK

Stop all this madness, cruelty barbarity,
You destroy yourselves, a pointless insanity.
With war of such kinds and weapons that devastate
Then there's construction, destruction the demons of real estate
You cut down the trees to make way for your motorway,
The rivers run green from the pollutants you throw away.
Then there is nuclear testing with God you are wrestling.
The power to kill with the flick of a switch.
Then media swarms to try take our minds away,
Children not sure of film or reality.
Death in our streets and death to our land,
We fear Armageddon yet give it a hand.
But did you ever once stop and just really think,
That we're on the edge almost over the brink.
This land it would prosper if it were not for man.
But kill our own planet and you will understand.
We cannot survive without her you see.
But she would survive without you or me.

R Chapman

FUTURE IMPERFECT

I met a horseman on the hill
And he was dressed in green
He said to me thou shalt not kill
The things that might have been

My green is for the fields of man
The grass now charred and brown
This King of beasts, this acid reign
What cost this tainted crown?

I met a horseman in the wood
And he was dressed in red
And on his head he wore a hood
And this is what he said

My red is for the blood of man
My hood so I can't see
The horse to take me far away
So I can then be free.

I met a horseman on the road
And he was dressed in black
I couldn't really see his eyes
Walk on and don't look back.

My black is for the death of man
Tomorrow his no longer
I've seen too much of his vain hand
And he will grow no stronger . . .

Gerard Martin

That's Now

We wandered over fields and hills
Picked blackberries and daffodils,
The morning air would always ring
With the chorus that the birds did sing,
Not *now*.

The blackberries are filled with lead,
The daffodils are long-since dead,
The birds have disappeared from view
'They' sprayed the land and killed them too,
That's *now*.

We used to wander many miles
Up the lanes and over stiles,
We paddled in the local stream
To catch a 'tiddler' was our dream,
Not *now*.

The lanes have gone we have the car
The motorways stretch near and far,
The streams have disappeared from view
The 'tiddlers' gone, the children too,
That's *now*.

The planet's on a downward trend
I wonder where it all will end,
'They' spray the land, pollute the air
And those in power seem not to care,
That's *now*.

B C Watts

Is There Still Time?

A precious, lovely, fragile gift He gave,
From formless void and chaos made the earth
With dawning life and finely balanced growth,
Slow age on age of wondrous change and birth,
God saw that it was good -
But evil lay in wait!

We tore the rainbow from the lofty sky
To drag it through a pool of filthy oil;
The quivering raindrops hid, in their deceit,
Hot burning acid, ready to despoil
This mutely dying land,
Abandoned to its fate.

Where rich green forests once gave shade and life
Bleak stumps and tortured branches pierce the air;
Fair meadows lie beneath our squalid waste
Poisoned, strangled, rotting in despair.
Our blame to see it all
Reduced to such a state.

Once food and home for little birds and beasts
Ancient hedgerows have been raped and killed;
By treacherous lure of weeds and crops well sprayed
The insects' hum and vibrant birdsong stilled,
Because of all our greed
And ignorance and hate.

The rivers, wells and shining, rolling seas
Cannot evade the ruin and the pain,
The tainted grasp and earth-destroying works
Of Adam's child, the everlasting Cain.
Lord, may we learn
Before it is too late!

Margaret Ballard

Man Losing Control. Stop. Anarchy Rife. Stop Destruction Imminent . . .

I come from a far distant planet, and mingle amongst you, unknown.
I make my reports and relay them back to the star system that
is my home.
Old civilisations I guided, was impressed by the progress they made;
my time I invested, great secrets divulged; my wisdom they
sought and obeyed.

But then hubris took over from wisdom; a Heaven was turning to Hell;
and the body of knowledge entrusted to man he used neither
wisely, nor well.
I had no choice but to destroy him, and to hide all the learning
I'd taught.
Now I've come back to see if you're ready once more for
advancement of life and of thought.

But I see here no progress - just decadence I find everywhere that I turn.
You maim and you kill; make good into ill; your peace plans to
ashes are burned.
Your sports, once noble, are shameful; you fight like mad dogs
in the street;
you destroy for a handful of money or drugs; your rulers they lie
and they cheat.

You've eschewed true wisdom, you meddle with nature, and toy,
interfere
with her laws, and the humble things you should protect are
wiser by far now, I fear.
They have feelings where you are insentient; and obedient
while you would run wild.
Thus you stand, each one guilty, yet denying your part in the
Treason of Order defiled.

J M Service

Tasmanian Tiger

From behind his prison bars
He yearned for his dignity
While cruel, hard people
Stood and stared.
Some will regret
Some will forget
They all know
Life's not fair.
He was never angry
He was truly beautiful
And preciously,
Sickeningly rare.
The world seems almost
Empty
Now I know
He's not there.

Debi Grant

By Permission Of Man

I heard the cry, or was it the moan
Of the elderly tree that now stood alone
Part of a family of the forest that breathed
Once life to the planet, but now no reprieve
The saw made a cut to the heart of that tree
Then all was so quiet, it was dead - not free
The birds had all flown, when the first trees did fall
No rustle of animal, no heartbeat at all
The life of the forest, is life no more
The murderer is man by the cut of the saw.

Mary Kathleen Mason

Our Heritage

Time and weather, both together,
Ensure that nothing lasts for ever.
The dust that in the wind doth blow,
Was once the hills of long ago.
Even the raindrops play a part,
Bringing to naught the mason's art.

Great tar ribbons cross the land,
Allowing our cities to expand.
No longer can we stand and stare,
Or stroke the muzzle of a mare.
There is not time, the pundits say
For anything that does not pay.

Yet much is saved from dissolution
By deep concern and resolution.
For crafts of old are precious history
Not to be lost in Time's dark mystery.
Thus it is up to us to strive
To keep our heritage alive.

Eileen McCappin

Newbury Bypass . . . Or Badgers' Sett?

How remiss the Highway Agency has been,
in its haste to plan, and build Newbury bypass.
English Nature even forbids them to *begin,*
to divert Old Brock's sett without their moving pass!
Badgers' mate, and rear, daily, new pied cubs within
nursery burrows, grubbed out soon, for the bypass.
Just this season, weaned young can forage for themselves -
but not where the road contractor meanly delves.

Gillian Fisher

UNTITLED

This planet holds no hope
For me.
We're destroying everything
Just wait
And see.
The future looks bleak.
We're killing all animals
We're killing all the trees.
Soon we'll be
Buying our oxygen
Over the counter
We have to breathe
You see.
We have to stop.
We have to cease.
We're destroying
Just wait
And see.

Maxene Huntley

HOPE FOR OUR PLANET

One has to live with nature so when will humans learn
To appreciate the gifts bestowed upon this precious earth,
Every creature has a purpose, each one has its place,
In the pattern of this living world all display their worth.

There's a cure for many ailments in every plant we're told
So why do we destroy them instead of taking care?
Deforestation is taking place at an alarming rate,
We have to stop this madness or wallow in despair.

Oil spills in the ocean put marine life under threat,
Pollution in the rivers disturbing habitat,
Wildlife struggling to survive through our greediness
Must halt the desecration before it is too late.

Aware of all the damage caused man is coming to his senses
Joining conservation groups with keen determination
With an optimistic outlook success can be achieved
Leaving a beautiful natural world for future generations.

D E Kowalska

POLLUTION

With every day
we ruin this place.
Slowly killing off
every living race.

With air pollution
its poisonous smoke.
Our planet earth
we do choke.

Chemicals in water
kill all fish life.
Just like they'd died
under our own knife.

To change our ways
it's not too late.
But what needs doing
just cannot wait.

J Muttock

This Is Not Science Fiction Anymore

This is not science fiction anymore . . .
Or some horror novel from which we can thankfully escape.

This is reality come to haunt us in all of its ugliness . . .
The gradual destruction of Mother Earth.

Environmental pollution by factories and by cars.
The overuse of manmade and synthetic products.
Contamination of all that we see;
And our bodies, our clothing.
Inside us, our food and our drink.

Yet as the world gets faster and we live on the run . . .
No *real* amount of pleasure is gained.
Grabbing all that we can . . .
Stealing, cheating, rat-racing . . .
Very few of us are not guilty.

To attain *more* and quickly
Or to become as unreal and as remote from our true nature as possible.

We are losing, not gaining . . .
For the Earth has turned upon us.
To wreak revenge for our savagery and crimes . . .
New illness, complicated and diverse.
Poisoning by pesticides, attacks on our immune systems,
dysfunction, mutations at birth . . .

Mankind has itself *only* to blame.

The world is dangerously plastic:
Out-gassing on us, killing us slowly . . .
And all we can do is to run about like seaside Punches.
Puppets with tempers and unhappy faces . . .
Beating others down, giving pain, and most of all, pain to our Mother.

Her mistake?
Allowing man to exist at all.

Laura Marchant

Our Precious Planet

What have we done to this world of ours,
With our chemical weapons and nuclear powers.
Mass genocide. Incessant wars.
Cruise missiles, the bomb that falls.

What have we done to this earth of ours,
with our modified Soya and engineered flowers.
Mutated plants. Pesticides which burn.
People that die in the midday sun.

What have we done to this globe of ours,
We destroy rain forests and make countless errors.
Vast cattle ranches. Torching the ground.
Digging for fuel but what have we found.

What have we done to this home of ours,
Decisions are made by political powers.
Famines, greed, man's desire
to ever push himself higher and higher.

What have we done to this planet of ours,
As time goes by the days become hours.
Push the button, will we or not?
But when it's finished, then what?

Audrey Maclean

CRIMES AGAINST THE PLANET

Man was made, born upon the Earth.
Evolution began.
Fossil fuels, supplies of energy made within the Earth's core.
Came to light.
And slowly, we have began to take these resources,
And use them to satisfy our own greed.
Creating a circle that will lead to our own ruin.
CFCs and gases damaged our ozone layer leaving a hole.
We stopped in time, many say.
And in our plight to stop the sun's rays we are working on a cure.
The rainforest is dying.
Hundreds of acres we lose every hour.
Many have opposed the chopping, but in vain!
Man has grown apart from each other,
From the Earth.
'Oh yes everyone else dumps their sewage in the waters, I will too.'
And Earth has struggled, tried to adapt to this,
But how can it carry on.
While all we do is take, giving nothing back.
Litter, junk, sewage, strewn about everywhere.
But do we care?
We believe it will be alright in the end.
But don't we realise, we've got to win this fight!

Carly Munday

WASTE

Abandoned land, now lying waste,
Weeds and garbage in control,
While green pastures fresh and chaste
Abused, take on a different role.

Logic too has been forsaken
Eating up the living earth,
While dead land lies to be awaken
And be given second birth.

Marguerite Yates

JUST THOUGHTS

Far too many inhabit this earth,
As we consider the control, of rate of birth.

Of food, for many, there is a dearth -
Others are greedy, just add to their 'girth'.

I'm not sure how it came to be,
But now we are plagued by BSE.

No one ever seems to care,
As cars pollute our daily fresh air.

Once we walked - got exercise,
Now we know it was very wise.

We would write a letter, when on our own,
Now we just pick up the telephone.

We use a machine, we can't 'add up',
Are we just getting out of touch?

Just a world of computers, more each day,
Do we know the price we will have to pay?

Just a few of the problems of our modern planet,
But is it any better? No, damn it!

Cindy White

How True:

How true mankind's crimes,
That never stop, they seem to go all times,
Crimes against this 'enchanting home',
This planet 'Earth' . . .
That from the beginning has 'great worth'.

There are places where trees once did be,
Woods and forest of grace, no more will we see,
Instead houses, shops, factories and new towns,
Where beauty was, lots have been chopped down:

Away from the coast whence you see light,
Not always ships but oil rigs working day and night,
Taking energy from waters below . . .
Like pumping the world's blood, it seems so:

Mankind has burrowed through caves,
Digging out coal and such,
Still people try to find treasures underground,
Think are these things making this 'world unsound':

Man never seems to stop . . .
About the dangers now, this world has got,
Why is this 'valid home' getting warmer,
And why lots of coastlines are being washed away:

We in this generation may not know,
But each and all will know one day,
There are they taking sand,
Nature's beauty that was once grand:

It all seems a shame . . .
Face facts each day naught is the same,
All mankind appears to look for . . .
Is materials things, that not always mean wealth,
All we seem to be doing is destroying the world's health:

Anita M Slattery

CIVILISATION

We still live today playing hunting games
Responding to our primitive instinct
We call it business among other names
Hard luck if more species become extinct

We all demand the best niche in the sun
At the expense of much weaker creatures
If they dare and rebel we use the gun
Or better still economic pressures

In geological terms we exist
A mere fraction of a flash. From birth
To death. Yet we obstinately persist
To make life a nightmare on this good Earth

Wasting valuable resources we enjoy
Fighting among ourselves to dominate
And in no time at all we destroy
What nature took eons to accumulate

We alter nature - so we can evolve
In a material way - till destruction
Creating more problems that we can resolve
And all in the name of civilisation

And we copulate, like rabbits we breed
We're told we cannot stop progress
We don't even notice in our blind greed
That our planet is in profound distress

And most of us go our little business
Having no time nor inclination to know
Through sheer ignorance or 'could not care less'
We live for today and damn tomorrow.

Jean-Claude Chandenier

WHEN YOU HURT YOUR MOTHER EARTH

When you cut
the trees
they cry
the tears
of innocent . . .

When you cut the throats
of these:
weak and meek ones
ignoring
their desperate
please
the skies are screaming
with the deepest
sorrow . . .

When you hurt
your Mother Earth
- you are killing
chance to live:
you are losing
your
Tomorrow.

Rorone

Man's Mindless Mess

Man's mindless mess.
Not designed to impress
Fish it and dish it up.
Cut squeeze and peel it.
Light it and burn it.
Mix it and stir it.
Slaughter cut pack freeze and stack it.
Man's mindless greed.
Intrusion pollution.
The better the wrecker.
Man with means on the fiddle.
Being first as the winner.
War want displaced people liberate exterminate.
Where's the caring and sharing.
Sun shrouded by clouds.
Planet earth is getting tired.
Crowded and crippled.
When there's nothing left to save.
Domination over God's creation.
Must we gaze and see it lost.
When knowing, it's worth so
'much'
Destroyers of the universe.
That's man's mindless mess.

Eileen Kay Gingell

God's World

The avarice in Man
Is blind to Earth's beauty
The beauty of Garden
God placed in his care,
And when God installed him
He told Adam 'Your duty,
is to keep ever fresh
All the wonderment here.'

But still there is time
to make restoration
Replace the good earth
that once filled the land,
To pull up the concrete
Return that perfection . . .
And show loving reverence
to our Maker's demand.

With love He created
Such beautiful nature
And sadly it dwindles
year after year . . .
Man blindly distorts
his own continuous future
With inedible concrete
That makes the land bare.

God's wonderful world
With its beautiful settings . . .
The rainforests, animals,
All the beautiful trees . . .
With time and tide merging
in true nature's fashion . . .
All these wonders of nature
Would remain ever free.

Mary Skelton

Message From Mother Earth

Cross-legged meditator . . . I
Go into the deep thought,
Of nothing in my mind.
Rooted to a spot . . . in trance,
Buried deep into the ground
Hear the message from Mother Earth . . . I.
Crying her heart out,
Into my buried roots.

My children,
Where did I go wrong?
What did I do wrong?
My little ones,
Why do you trample on me,
With so much anger?
Disrespect me with your hate.
Can we sit down . . . talk,
Let's go back, start anew.
Come back to me.

My children,
The way you were born . . . naked.
We can renew our love once again.
My little ones,
I need you as you need me.
I have always loved you.
Do not turn on me,
So come . . . talk . . . children,
My little ones.

Kiran Shah

Dinosaurs And Stone Age Men

Rugged, jagged, twisting forms
All made up the world adorned -
With dinosaurs, Stone age men
Roaming around the planet when -
The only meal they had was killed
Not for greed not for thrills
just to stay alive to succeed
in sowing the future's natural seed
Man just used what God had to give
The food of nature, how to live,
Now there's nothing but greed and violence
No more harmony, no more silence,
Can we get back to the way we were
Or will life become one big blur,
Dinosaurs, Stone Age men
Roamed this planet way back then.

Susan Askew

Our World

The world is mad with greed and sin
Men fight, and hate, and kill
Christ walks unheeded through the streets
A man of sorrows still
He sees with grief, the human race
Still squirming in the mud
And through his tears, he sees the earth
Defiled and drenched with blood
Man strives to conquer, dominate
And take the place of God
The world would be a beautiful place
If men could live in harmony
Within the human race.

Bill Williamson

IS THIS THE ANSWER

The reassuring tides of fate
Flowed slowly back and forth -
Nature's pattern never changed
Proving what living was worth.

Now this old dying planet -
Reels from violence and strife -
Some say it's the Devil's kingdom -
Wielding Satan's sharp knife.

Grannies battered, children abused
The cowards choose their victims -
Nations at war, their people starving -
Fact is stranger than fiction.

And just when we feel we can take no more
We witness the black tide of doom
Unleashed by that filthy oil spill
Stark silhouettes against the moon.

Harbour seals, otters and sea birds
Innocents, each one of them -
Choking and dying, covered in sludge
Once again the victims of men.

We hear of dedicated people
Working tirelessly against gales and tide
Rescuing those helpless creatures.
Compassion is their guide.

Do these things happen for a reason
To teach us to soften our thoughts?
All of us feel *pity* -
So a lesson we've been taught!

Mary Armstrong

Some Devil May Smile

We rape and take and
Poison with fusion and fire
Like dominoes falling these scenes
Of childhood dreams
Shall wither and blow away
In the blink of an eye
Under ancient sky
The fate of this world is decay
To build, to eat and to reproduce
We fell and kill and burn
To travel the web and heal our heads
We fell and kill and burn
To search the stars and comfort our pride
We fell and kill and burn
Through tiny vessels the chaos leaks
Tainting this creation
Like a cancer we spread
The earth is bled
We seek to our end
Oblivion
We do not bite, but
Sever the hand that feeds us.

Kelvin Mayes

Man's Destruction

For centuries on planet earth
since discovery by man,
our planet is still plundered,
to increase the wealth of man.

With North Sea gas and oil fields
being sucked from planet earth,
and now deforestation, with fires
that contaminate our world.

With nuclear bombs that blast
through earth's gigantic core,
are now't compared with earth's reserve,
a giant volcanic roar.

With a future land restriction
caused by swelling seas,
from man's misuse of chemicals,
we will bring planet earth upon its knees.

John Hickman

NUCLEAR CHESS

Twin towers rise above the plain
One of pain, one of joy,
Death and destruction in the clouds;
What hope is there for girl and boy?

Horizon heaves as though of dust,
Brown grass, black leaves unfurl,
Birds fly upon the ground;
What hope is there for boy or girl?

Sweat on the brow, blood on the hand,
Man plays with lethal toys
Torturing his planet;
What hope for girls and boys?

Flies to the moon
His flags to unfurl,
Looks next to the sun;
What hope for boy or girl?

Twin pillars on the horizon
One of dust, one of flame,
Man has bought the sun to earth;
Boy and girl will not have birth.

Arthur J Pullen

Land Of Tears

Bent and broken, drowning in salt water
once a green and happy land
bows its knee before the apathy of its people

Pastures once filled with ripe golden corn
nourished by rain falling so sweet
are now parched and scorched fields
which yield nought but sorrow and starvation

Where once flew brightly coloured birds
singing sweet songs in the lush green forests
now stand only gaunt blackened skeletons
of what were once royal oaks

Where once red admirals fluttered gently by
on purple-headed clover rich
lie only stark horizons with lifeless air
choking the breath from the brave new world

Where lambs skipped and gambolled merrily
skeletal beasts scratch dead soil for non-existent food

Where once children played and skipped and sang
now lies the dust and rubble of houses broken by
the men who love to hate;
the women who fear to love

Where once was peace and harmony
hate and fear have broken in
to each pure heart a barb has flown
and smashed the arrows of love and joy

To this land of mighty hills;
tallest trees; deepest seas;
has come the wailing and beating of breasts.

Fiona Higgins

CRIMES AGAINST THE PLANET

'Planet earth has been here for millions of years' -
Well now, that's a crime for a start!
'Twas God who created this universe vast
Of which planet earth is a part.
Just thousands, not millions, of years have gone by,
Since He first created the earth and the sky.

Man descended from monkeys, or so we are told;
Is that why like beasts we behave?
Rejecting the moral and natural laws
Which God for our benefit gave.
'Replenish the earth and subdue it,' He said,
But we have contrived to destroy it instead.

Since first we began to launch things into space,
Weather patterns have not been the same.
No more long, hot summers, or deep winter snow;
Just rain, and more rain, and more rain!
We've polluted our rivers, polluted the seas,
We've even polluted the air that we breathe.

The creatures that live in our habitats wild
May soon be extinct; but who cares?
And what of our children, and those still to come?
Just what sort of world will be theirs?
A world that's been almost destroyed by our greed;
And why? We've already got more than we need.

Where cattle once grazed in the wide open fields,
Large housing estates now we see.
Where people once lived, ugly office blocks stand;
Ghastly blots on the landscape they be.
Never mind about Mars, or any other planet;
Life on earth can't be very intelligent, can it?

D J Mackay

CRIME TO WAKE UP

Crime does not tell the truth
Yet truth shows the consequences.
Here on earth man has lied;
Misplaced true worth, and valued
Millennium Dome follies
Fat cats' insurance policies
High stocks and shares,
Braggarts who act in self-interest,
Who sell their souls to fashion flare;
Money driven demon gods
Who pollute the air.
Here on earth man kills
In thoughtless choices.
Wrong deeds, etch coverings of excuses
Concealing the cry within
For sharing, equal in everything.
We have lost real relationship,
Lost the central jewel
And traded in our unique contributions
For selfish, dim-witted, me-grabbing profusions.
And through this sorrow-ridden world
One command is clear;
To learn the route back home:
Wake up! Wake up I hear.

Marion Elvera

People and Planet?

The Earth has been revolving for millions of years,
A balance between life and death,
The natural cycle of life,
A mutual respect between all creatures,
The world in perfect harmony.
Years later human beings were born
With all their hatred and greed,
Nothing was ever enough for them,
They always wanted to kill one more animal
Not for food but for vanity.
They were too lazy to put their rubbish in a bin,
Too lazy to walk anywhere,
Too greedy to spend money on CFC-free sprays
Or organic fruit and vegetables,
Too ignorant to believe they could make a difference.
But that is all it will take to make a better planet,
For us all to make a slight change,
A bit more effort.
We can't undo the damage we've already done,
But if we can learn by our mistakes
We can stop replicating them
Over and over again,
And maybe this world,
And us,
Stands half a chance.

Lindsey Brown

KEEP THE PLANET HEALTHY

Listen! Can you hear the message that's echoing
around the world?
Of the fight to save the planet and the costly
lessons learned.
The earth is dying we are warned, over-heating
and pollution.
The greenhouse effect and acid rain, the ozone layer
and global pain.
Thousands starve while food mountains grow the Third World
needs wheat and grain.
Giant tankers spill their oil and pollute the world's
seas and oceans.
Giant problems for the world's leaders to solve with
the United Nations.
But what of the issues closer to home, just what
is to be seen?
Of our contribution to keep the planet healthy,
what has this been?
Lead-free petrol is an encouraging sign, less
air pollution
Recycling of paper, glass and cans is helpful to
the solution.
Sprays, asbestos and lead-based paints are being
banned at last.
Conservation of woodlands and wildlife helps to
protect our past.
Greenpeace and *the friends of the earth* and others
wage the fight.
To keep the planet healthy for our children, which is
their own birthright.

Terry Daley

WHERE HAVE ALL THE FIELDS GONE?

Shimmering haze over golden field,
Sun blessed corn with crop to yield.
Seldom's there a more beautiful sight,
Than a field of corn bathed in sunlight.
Such a spectacle that's sure to please,
As heads of corn sway in the breeze.
Heads wrapped tightly clothed in green,
Full of goodness as yet unseen.
Skylarks singing up above,
Whilst pigeons coo their song of love.
Such a treat for ears and eyes,
With blazing sun filling cloudless skies.
A kestrel hovers, alert in wait,
For a careless vole to seal its fate.
Its movements seen the kestrel drops,
On unsuspecting prey hidden by the crops.
No chance for little creature to run and hide,
Just one little movement made its death warrant signed.
A once common scene, seen less and less,
As fields are covered by an urban mess.
Will it only end when all the fields are gone?
When bricks and mortar appear to have won.
If that happens we'll all have lost,
And we'll never be able to repay the cost.
Do we really need to build and build,
And watch silently, Mother Nature killed.
There'll be nowhere left for generations to come,
To sit and watch nature in the sun.
With no sun blessed corn with crop to yield,
They haven't even left the field.

David Ford

BREATHE IN THE AIR

First in the day there was night
Then in the night there came the light
People danced with crystals in their eyes
Too many nights within the day
People moaned, confusion reigned
Mother's way to nature's end, she cried

People turned to breathing gold
Sold their souls rich when they're old
Nothing matters more than what they see
Never mind the dying earth
They take her now for what she's worth
Turn away from the reality they breathe

Breathe in the air, you have to
Breathe in the air

Take a mouthful of what you need
Clean your mind and sow the seed
Nothing matters more than what you feel
Time will tell if this is hell
It is if you're prepared to sell
Visions of the truth inside you feel

Breathe in the air, you have to
Breathe in the air

The earth, she cries from within
Calling out to tame our sins
Crying out to change the way we live
Breathe in the air 'cause it'll take you there
Love the crystal in your hair
Love yourself, love the earth and give, and

Breathe in the air
You have to
4

Vincent Rees

THE END OF OUR WORLD

Towards the end of a busy day
In an even busier life,
I make the time to contemplate
And think about the crazy state
Of the world in which we live and breathe
For the end of our world is nigh.

And thoughtless man in his endless quest
For an even bigger prize
Must take the time to understand
That all the trees chopped down by man
In this world in which we live and breathe
Makes the rest of our world capsize.

Man's greed prevents all healthy construction
Before our very eyes.
We must put a stop to this wanton destruction
Before our planet dies.

Helen Strangwige

Mankind

A grain of sand on the desert of time.
A drop in the ocean of life.
More like a spanner that clogged up the works.
A disease that is running rife.

The water got into the hourglass
and disrupted the normal flow.
If he can't put right, nature's ordered plan,
it will soon be time to go.

When man has gone he will leave his mark,
to show his wisdom and worth.
Not a harmless footprint in the sand,
but boils on the face of the earth.

Boils, that were caused by an ugly disease,
that destroys, defaces, decays.
A disease called greed, that should have been lanced
and the poison washed away.

If the verdict for treason is guilty,
for crimes against this earth.
Should he be allowed to spread his wings
and infect the whole universe?

Coral Dranfield

Mink Escape!

When those protesters let us out,
our Christmas Day had come,
But six weeks down the line and now
life isn't all that fun.

New Forest folk were told they could
shoot any mink on sight,
The noise those farmers' rifles make
force us all to take flight.

So pellets fly above our heads,
and food's in short supply,
Whichever way we turn it seems
us mink are bound to die!

If we'd stayed there and met our fate
we'd still have got the chop,
So we shout loud for all to hear,
'When will this madness stop?'

Peter Ranscombe (16)

To The Brothers And Sisters Of Light

Men laugh, men joke, men drink, men smoke
to bear the burden of the yoke that binds them to this world.

Men laugh, men cry, men live, men die,
to reach their ends they'll cheat and lie, regardless of the price.

Who hears God cry as children die?
Who feels His pains as violence reigns?
Indeed who heeds as nature bleeds, her laws confused, awry?

So great then is man's need for power,
so deep his sense of fear, so blind his understanding
as to why he's really here.

And yet like gems amidst the stone, or gold within dark lead,
around the world new life is found where life and hope seemed dead.

And those with hearts alive with Light, with purpose that is real,
are surely coming back again to build - to bridge - to heal.

And hands reach out and touch and clasp across this aching sphere,
as friendship based on Love and Trust replaces hurt and fear.

Scarlett

SHETLAND SEALS

Large moist eyes
like dark glass
glisten sadly
now that they mourn
a spoiled world.
Their sleek shapes slip
into sticky blackness
ballet dance through
storm-swelled waves
unknowing that oily poison
wraps their gliding forms
twisting graceful movements
into agony until
too weak to swim
they lie in fear and pain
trying to blink away
the stinging blindness
from shining eyes.

Helen Clarke

QUESTION

Ah, Modernity, what is your will?
To stink my water
With cloying of chlorine
So I daren't drink my fill?

Ah, Modernity, what is your will?
To drench your fields
With bird deadly sprays
Which go in for the kill?

Ah, Modernity, what is your will?
To belch from your vehicle,
Cause the sky to unwhole,
Warn we all may be still?

Ah, Modernity, what is your will?
Can you hear me call
Above your roaring machines:
How may your heart fill?

Solomon Blue Waters

SUBSEQUENT HIROSHIMA

Gazing upon the bare ground,
lacking any sign of life,
death dominating, revelling in its victory.

A glimmer of light chanced upon a golden frame.
A surge of vitality and life amongst death,
beauty laughing in the face of ugliness,
denying all humane possibilities
and proving the pessimists wrong.

Happiness is short lived,
aspirations crushed
for the living object was surreal.

The butterfly landed, struggling to release
its seven misshapen wings.

Deformity the conqueror
pessimists grin in sadistic joy.

Gemma Bowen

BEYOND THE BRINK

As nation's wars become replaced
By nature's angry voice.
As roarings of the tides give vent
With spleen upon her choice.

Her reign of terror thus engulf
As mankind bows its head.
To lose the precious gift of life
Upon an ocean bed.

As rivers dry, where no birds sing
All occupation still.
To late for those as yet unborn
To answer to its trill.

As deserts creep with stealthy tread
And climates ebb and flow
With distant cries from those unfed
And water's gift turned low.

Will mankind heed these warning drums
And strive to turn the sway?
Or rest within cocoon-like life
To live another day.

Tick-tock, will beat this planet's clock
With time's relentless flow.
How long before all else is lost
Will mankind ever know?

Joan G Railiffe

Please Leave Us Our Trees

Trees grow upwards as they search for light,
to see sun and sky they have to fight,
In forests world-wide the trees grow tall,
but alas in time to man they will fall.

For years on end each tree grows high,
in its quest to reach the clear blue sky,
The higher the sky the longer the length,
the longer the time the greater the strength.

Through sun and rain, wind and snow,
each tree in the forest continues to grow,
To wildlife it's home, their own sanctuary,
in fact it's more, 'tis their kitchen pantry.

Alas good timber grows only on trees,
and man and machine can get it with ease,
Chainsaws roaring, then it's 'Timber' they cry,
sadly another tree fails to reach that blue sky.

Those beautiful trees which looked up to the stars,
now lay with broken branches, their man-made scars,
Soon to be dismembered and sent to the saw mills,
to be turned into paper, or doors, frames and sills.

The world must stop this rape and pillage,
of forests that neighbour the rural village,
Man's plundered oil in the deserts and seas,
enough is enough; please leave us our trees.

Wenn-The-Penn

Crimes Against The Planet

How long can we pollute this world
before it breaks.
How much more of our
tearing down border lines
of destruction
will it take?
Why can't we keep this place together
by using a little grace.
What next?
Who can tell?
Who can say?
Except the one who made this day.
I don't believe it's up to us
to wreck this planet,
but it is up to us to take care,
if we don't want it to fall
back to granite!

Naomi Elisa Price

Destroying Our Earth

They're building on land now,
  That once was covered by the sea,
So no wonder the tides are coming in,
  In places they never used to be.

They're also building on ground
  Where our forests used to be,
In fact you can drive for miles now
  Without seeing a single tree.

They're burning plastic in incinerators,
  Putting poisonous gasses in the air,
No wonder it causes damage
  To the ozone layer.

This is supposed to be 'progress'
  But I think man is going too far,
'Cos he pollutes the planet daily,
  Releasing petrol fumes from his car.

Jean Hendrie

WORLD PEACE

Religion on one side.
Reality on another.
They both point to the
common-sense of
world peace.

Green issues are essential,
or there'll be no material
for building those
homeless shelters.

Recycling rubbish
for making lab materials
is necessary for the
World Brotherhood:
and sensible management
of resources for the future.

Keith Murdoch

Playground

Where do we go from here on this roundabout of extremes
Where one man's nightmare can be another man's dreams
With little fellowship or a warm embrace
Freely given without cost to the human race
When one child can be born within love and joy
Another thrown away like a broken toy
How much longer will we find a corner green and clean
That's not watered by rain full of gangrene
When we are told our planet is dying
We express some concern but are we really trying
To change our fate would show some distinction
Or like the big ones will be face extinction
If this is truly a playground for us to learn
I watch uneasy, with sadness and great concern.

S E Spooner

Memories Of An Evacuee

Six years of childhood buried in this place,
A childhood interrupted by a war,
A small Somerset village, off the face
Of a map, to me opened welcome doors.
Immersed in country folk, ways and beauty,
I grew cocooned in family love and care,
A father at war doing his duty,
Sure I was safe evacuated there.
My world then simple - flowers, birds and trees,
Milking cows, country walks, hay harvesting,
Growing in my garden, beans, lettuce, peas,
Making jam after blackberry picking.
Sixty years on, a visit yields no trace
Of these memories in my heart encased.

Pat Heppel

FRAGMENTS

Most old places will have them,
Some hidden some bold; with stories of yesterdays -
Yet to be told, scatterings of old walls
Not labelled it's true, but parts of the boundaries
From yesterday's youth.

Where are our boundaries now to be found, destroyed and
Forgotten, not on the ground; nothing stable or firm
For young people to hold; to grasp and keep,
Knowing this won't be sold.

Sold like the rain falling down from the skies;
Fruits of the earth; there for us to find
Not a thing is for free, just the sight from our eyes -
And the song of the birds, that our ears glorify.

Forests uprooted to satisfy greed, unthinking people
Who will not heed; warnings of death of this
Wonderful world; as their coffers fill, will our earth go cold . . .

Blow away on the wind, with no rain from the sky -
The balance all wrong; as the greedy defiled;
There is goodness still there; fragments still to be found;
Can we stop them in time, plant their feet on the ground.

All working together with love as the head, love for all
Of the beauty, our pathways to tread;
To leave behind sureness, not fragments of walls -
Peace; love for each other, and all of mankind.

Peggy Morrill

Greed

Millions of years our planet Earth has spun,
A tiny speck, around the parent sun.
Uniquely lovely, to what mystic end
Pulsing with life we scarcely comprehend.
Slowly developed, shaped by ice and fire,
Its balance all that plants and men require.
Till - springing first perhaps from simple need -
Mankind let loose the poison of its greed.
'Thou shalt not covet . . .' ancient wisdom said.
'I want, so I will have,' we cry instead.
Heedless of suffering, undeterred by strife,
With greedy hands we clutch our planet's life.
Rainforests fall, we poison sea and sky,
And all around our meadows and hedgerows die;
Nor can we plead, 'We did not understand,'
But heedless, heartless, devastate our land,
And those who seek to save our planet's face
At times seem shouting into empty space.
Our greed will be our death unless we wake
And learn compassion for our planet's sake.
Freedom of will is ours, as foes or friends -
Oh man! Cast off your greed and make amends.

Kathleen M Hatton

Man Strikes Again

Yet still, man has not realised
  A disaster happened yesterday
A disaster of such scale and size
  It will affect the whole world wide

The oil that is spewing out
  It kills all that it meets
The otters, the birds, the seals
  And all the fish that they eat

How can man be so stupid?
  Why does he not realise?
What lessons did he learn and forget
  When it happened the last time?

Why can't man think of what he does?
  Why must mistakes be repeated?
Will he only realise when it's too late
  Then to whom will he cry and bleat

  Since it's man's own doing.

K Arblaster

A Recipe For Disaster

Dump your refuse into the sea
Kill all aquatic life you see.
Chop down forests and make barren the land
Nothing will grow on just plain sand.
Poison the air with your toxic fumes
And send your rockets up to the moon.
If it's thicker smog that you require
Use leaded gas, burn coal on your fire.
The hole in the ozone will heat up the globe
And melt the great icebergs until the seas overflow.
Now spray your crops with DDT
No insect will live, not even a bee.
Hundreds of animals cannot survive
They must eat these creatures to remain alive.
With no butterflies or bees to fertilise the crop
There will be no rejuvenation, no next year's stock.
Now place your disaster under the sun's unprotected rays
And watch as the landscape goes up in a blaze.
You have now achieved according to plan
This wasted disaster created by man.

Rose Mulligan

THE GARDENERS

We wanted to kill the grub that was attacking the apple trees
forgetting we'd kill other insects, butterflies and bees.
Last year there were real robins - not just on a Christmas card
but the sprays we used and weed killers made its survival too hard.
Instructions were 'spray this on the lawn and watch the moss turn
brown it is harmless to creatures' we were told but the earthworms
carried it down,
down into the deeper earth as they ventilated the soil
- birds love eating earthworms, we've all watched them as they toil
as they tug and pull at an earthworm which we now know can kill
the robin and also, eventually, poisons will travel and spill
down through the earthworm tunnels and thus into our rivers
where fish will feed and die of our poisons, we're the givers.
Now we've got pretty apple trees and grass with no moss at all
but where oh where are the robins? Over everything hangs this pall
of silence. No birds are singing upon the apple bough
and you'd hardly know if you were in England in April now.
The robin is just a memory - forever it is lost
but people persist in their folly however high the cost.
The Bible says 'not a sparrow falls but our heavenly Father knows'
what about fallen robins that no longer brighten our snows?
Soon we'll have to pay the price for the sin of this mass killing
Is there really a death-wish that is also self fulfilling?
We can't kill any living thing with no thought for tomorrow
Tomorrow may well be too late for us to show our sorrow
What can we say to our children when all the robins are gone
'We didn't care enough my child - my daughter and my son -
so we can't pass on the robins and the other birds-of-song
Fish are dead, birds are dead, we've done you and them a wrong
With a bit more air pollution there won't be enough snow
for the robin to have stood on if we hadn't made it go!

F B Broomfield

The Planet Earth

As human beings
We can't seem to see
The state of our planet
And how it should be
We are gradually destroying
Our whole country life
Where the factory waste
Is the worst kind of blight
Seeping to rivers and into
the sea
Killing the fish
All the plankton and weeds
Aerosol sprays, exhaust fumes
from cars
Affecting our children
Wherever they are
Burning up forests
And cutting down trees
It all seems to stem
From incredible greed
The warnings are grim
Global warming still grows
The rivers are rising
Soon to overflow
We should heed we must
For our future's at stake
We must do something now
Before it's too late

Jeanette Gaffney

WATERWORLD

Such heat, how it parched the land,
turning rich moist earth to grains of sand,
my eyes so old, in youth saw grow,
colourful flowers under glorious rainbows,
The greatest, down to the smallest,
all the animals that roamed free,
drowned under a merciless rising sea,
out of melting ice caps,
our waterworld was slowly born,
harsh punishment, ignoring nature,
we were constantly warned.

How I miss from my youth,
wonders, of which, I could freely see,
green grass, barley fields, deserts so bare,
mountains and forest, nature's glory everywhere,
seasons of change, bronzed leaves,
The freshest purest whitest snow,
all of summer's sweet scents, spring's first glow,
fresh morning dew, cold drops of rain,
birds of the world, I wish to see fly again,
our greed inspired destruction,
ensured for God's creation of all,
The end of the world.

Elaine Hawkins

IN THE EVENT OF NUCLEAR WAR (PROTECT AND SURVIVE)

Thus I read while taking tea
'And should a mushroom cloud you see
Behind a suitcase hide and be
Irradiated dead and free.'

Nicholas Howard

THIS EARTH OF OURS

This Earth of ours, oh Lord we pray,
Look after trees and flowers today.
The birds and animals with no soul,
Suffer from pain that we could control.

Allow each growing thing a place,
Upon the earth that we each do grace.
Tend nature's needs with love and care
And in return, seeds they will bear.

With love and patience we will find,
Peace, contentment, flowing in mind.
Please God watch over all your land,
For this world requires a wise old hand.

Protect and guard all nature's treasures,
That we destroy in our selfish leisure.
Give us strength to use all our senses,
To appreciate beauty without fences.

The roots inherent in all our being,
Should provide understanding, an all seeing.
To watch and wonder as beauty unfolds,
So protect and nurture world-old moulds.

For this is the world that God gave to us,
So why do we have a need to possess?
Tender please all living creatures,
Including flowers and all earth's features.

Kerry D Beck

I Wish

What's that over there dear?
A what? A tree, are you sure?
Ah yes I can see now,
We just don't see them anymore.

These masks work fairly well,
Though they make a mess of my hair,
But to wear them is a must,
Or we'd die from having no air.

I'm glad we kept those books,
Else people will never believe us,
The fauna and the flora we had,
Before man's greed became contagious.

Yes these books will show them,
What a lovely planet we had,
The flowers, the colour, the landscapes,
All gone now, oh it makes me sad.

Oh well dear, come along,
Looking back will do us no good,
Nothing at all we can do now,
But oh how I wish we could.

Glennis Horne

The Phoenix Rising

Wanton man's destruction stands
casting outward everything
waste and broken wishes
and all thoughts of being free.

Would not all who brought the darkness
come again a new regime
altered faces in abundance
heard but never seen.

Mounds of ash where once stood
all of man's achievements dying
carried on the acid wind
mother earth diseased.

Return again then if you can
anew the phoenix rising
a new beginning for the few
a fresh perception seen.

Tony Megson

Atomic Poker

Atomic poker, a world wide game,
That could end up with atomic rain.
A deck of cards, a shuffled pack,
Once it's dealt, there's no going back.
No discarding or re-deal,
The consequences are too real.
Aces high, a poker face,
When the cards are dealt, there's no hiding place.
Diamonds, hearts, clubs or spades,
The pack is cut, the cards are laid.
Each poker player holds a hand,
He thinks he'll win, his game is planned.
Cards kept close against the chest,
Won't reveal the one that's best.
Bluff and counter bluff takes place,
Who holds the king? The queen? The ace?
There's no knowing till it's laid,
Just who will win the game that's played.
Around the world, atomic poker,
We pray there's no atomic joker!

Jim Sargant

CRAWLING MONSTER

You are a lecherous city,
Crawling out of town,
Raping all the countryside,
For miles and miles around.

Motorways like tentacles,
Stretching far away,
Scaring all the countryside,
Cutting into clay.

Fumes pollute the country air,
Litter lines the lane,
The cities sprawl is spreading,
Just like an angry flame.

Well-groomed urban houses,
In state of disrepair,
Owners that don't bother,
People that don't care.

Vandals wreak their havoc,
In the twilight zones,
All the city dwellers,
Are prisoners in their homes.

You are a wicked city,
Full of greed and sloth,
Gobbling up the countryside,
Like a malignant growth.

You big industrial city,
Eating up your host,
Soon you'll spread all over England,
Engulfed from coast to coast.

J E Sharpe

When The World Was Left To Die

As I walked alone through the streets of the city
There was a stillness and a calm;
A silence filled with a cry of pity
And I felt the sweat in my palm.

Concrete monsters rose up from the skyline
Where man was replaced by machine;
Steel fingers that worked with relentless precision
Till man was extinct from the scene.

No light was there or laughter so gay,
'Twas gloomy and forlorn.
No creature heard I on my walk
As if no beast were born.

I wandered on in hope to find
A person such as I,
Alone and full of heartache
When the world was left to die.

When madness had possessed us all,
Where had mankind gone wrong?
To rob the children of their youth,
The robin of its song.

The parish church was empty,
And in the pulpit there
I stood and thought of all my sins
And offered up a prayer.

Please God release us from this urge
To worship gold and steel;
And make the night, I walked alone
A nightmare, never real.

Sylvia Brice

ARROGANCE

When human beings, of all things living,
Have the power of thought and reasoning,
Why can't they understand the rhyme,
That life on earth must intertwine?

Arrogantly we stand apart,
When aren't we just a tiny part
Of nature's glorious work of art -
The living planet earth?

Long ago how well we knew,
The laws which nature links us to,
But now, with crass temerity,
We see her as our enemy.

King of all beasts; chief of all clans,
Above all else we say we stand,
And yet, the earth with our demise,
Would go on living, would survive.

In blinkered mind we crave for power,
For wealth and all we can devour,
And say what value can there be,
In birds and beasts and flowers and trees?

It's right, we think, to multiply,
To live forever, not to die,
But earth will not sustain the load,
And nature then must cull the herd.

And in the lead up to that day,
What tortures suffer on the way?
What legacy we leave our child?
A barren earth, a broken world?

Upon all life mankind depends,
With nature we must make amends,
Preserve the earth's abundant treasure,
And only then survive forever.

So let us end our selfish greed,
We have enough, no more we need,
We cannot take and not return,
For earth was never ours alone.

Joan Robson

We Don't Know It's There

Keep digging, down, down,
Deeper, deeper in the ground,
Dump them in, pack 'em tight,
No-one knows what's happened tonight.
'Cover them good' 'Pat down the dirt'
What people don't know
Won't hurt.
Down deep, in the ground,
A hissing sound, an acid smell,
The Earth is burning,
It will be hell.
Stop them doing this, killing our Earth,
Dumping night after night,
Let's make a stand, together we can fight,
Wake up, look around, see the damage in our ground.
Mother Nature needs our help,
Don't let her fight in vain,
Let's all of us unite.
Go *Green*
And ease her crying pain.

K Moon

Blue

We know more about the Moon
Than the deep, briny blue,
But ignorance is no excuse
For the sea's continued abuse.
From the spilling of black fuel
That to seabirds is so cruel,
To the dumping of human waste
Which washes up all over the place,
The oversize fishing nets
That lead to dolphin deaths,
To catching too much fish;
I have one simple wish.
Stand up and make a commotion
About the spoiling of oceans
Before the worst of our fears
Lead to a sea of tears.

Andrew Fisher

Our Earth

This planet is ours,
not yours, or theirs.
So what have you done to it?
Doesn't anyone care?
Nuclear testing.
Resources extracting.
Stripped by more than one or two.
Destroy it then, why don't you?
Then we will see,
there'll be nothing left,
for you or for me.

Susan J MacDonald

War On A World

When the power of the sun to earth was flung
By the immature hand of Man
A song of peace was brokenly sung,
And the world breathed another span.
But everything changed within the range
Of nuclear poisoned breath,
And all that remained was a silhouette
Of a city enmeshed in death.

But was this the end of human dread?
No, just the beginning, it seems.
Bigger and more destructive bombs shed
Their havoc in skies, seas and streams.
As Cold War terror engulfed earth's mind
Under nations' experiments
Our atmosphere simmered in toxic drifts,
Irradiated elements.

In these days our planet has still not found peace;
Global warming and acid rain,
Stunted forests and deserts' increase
Were not part of nature's plan.
The trees that nourish our world with life
Are mercilessly hacked down;
This is not a season for apathy -
The seeds of destruction are sown.

Pamela Harvey

Crimes Against The Planet

The title of this poem is interesting to a degree.
But the true, and myths about this world I disagree.
Man as always been the scapegoat for this earth's decline,
But nature itself scars the earth which is supposed to be sublime.
The violence of the wind, tide, volcanoes
Are destructive powers, beyond compare.
When man meets these forces, it is wise for him to take great care.
If one spoon of water was taken from a village pond, on a warm summer's day,
Under a microscope would show a life and death display.
When nature's forces cause despair, the comparison between nature and man is so unfair.
Man's deeds have helped this destruction and decay.
But without man, this destruction would only have been delayed.
Nature is not a compassionate force, it lets the strong survive.
Man's combat with nature is the reason why he's still alive.

T G J Sutton

Elysium's Passing

This was once green
Once green, smelling of leaf and wood, petal and flower
Once green, quietly rustling, birdsong and squirrels chattering.

Then brown with churned mud, punctuated by the yellow of JCBs
Then brown, cacophonies of construction during the day, deathly hush at night.

Now grey, concrete and asphalt
Now grey, the only animals to be seen are cats' eyes and road kill
Now grey, filled with impatient motorists, fumes, thoughtless litter
Now grey, Elysium made Pandemonium.

Al Treacher

Pure Earth

Dream a distant far off world
originally perhaps new planet earth
freshly moulded pollution-free globe rotating
blue suspended orb on starry speckled infinity background
and watch it grow . . .

the seeds of life in a large beautiful ocean
from which lethargic land masses groggily appear
crawling from underwater sea depths
dragging bleary-eyed creatures with them
giant seaweed steps for animal-kind

glints of brilliant sunshine twinkle
off the surface of clear spring water
shallow reflections of soft clouds and magnificent trees
bobbing lightly from the fresh cool breeze

a scene idyllic and tranquil
touched only by the gentle loving hand of Mother Nature
dusted and polished, clean and pure
a peaceful relaxed sun-trap
made ready for its first night

the sun tucks itself into bed
and a calm warm atmosphere hangs silently over the planet
broken only by insects clicking away at the tangerine skyline
undisturbed, unspoilt and blissful
evolve, but beware the seventh day

Amen

Steve Warner

THE MOTORWAY

The old house no longer stands on the majestic drive:
willing hands tore it apart after years of sheltering.
Children's voices echo amongst the moon silvered wastes:
as dawn light shadows the space where once dreams that were real;
hung on crooked nails behind closed doors.
The lost days of childhood whisper through the jumbled haze of
rattling lorries: mumbled conversations settle like brick dust on
mechanical shovels.
Looking back are we merely part of the shifting background of
change: bound forever by the uncertainty of belongings?
Will they ever forgive us those children whose spirits haunt the
concrete rivers like will-o-the wisps?
Would they take our hand and say of us; 'We understand. You did
what you could?'

Chris Senior

CRUELTY OF MAN

All over the world such cruelty is shown,
man's brutality to animals is now well-known.
Majestic elephants, killed just for their tusks,
rhinoceros' horns ground down to their husks.
Rainforests destroyed, where trees once stood high
with their habitat gone, so many will die.
Beasts of burden so laden and thin
submissive and beaten, they know they can't win.
Animals in cages with no room to turn round,
heart-rending scenes that never cease to astound.
Creatures who are slaughtered because they are too many
but no-one controls man, who are ten-to-a-penny.

Carole Bloomfield

It's My Earth As Well

Twisted, bitter and always damaged
The planet earth, well I'm disgusted.
We've pilfered and punished the virgin ground
I'm not even sure that this earth is round.
We've dug and destroyed what was given at birth
There's nothing left of our sacred earth.
We've structured nature to look like concrete
Killed off trees, flowers and clean breeze.
I cannot give up, I'm not beat
I'll save this land before I leave.
I want to be buried in the soil
Not burnt and scattered in pools of oil.
So release this earth and make the punishment stop
Just take time, stand and study our rock.
Foundations we stand on, are not yet unstable
We can save this earth, we all are able.

Ann Taplin

The Vanishing Land

For many summers I walked the same footpath,
Where dandelions and wild poppies grew,
And I felt much brighter in my mind and heart,
When I saw the meadow browns and chalk-hill blue.

But one day ill-fortune played a cowardly card,
And cut through my idyll cold and hard,
Building machinery was all around,
Destroying that beautiful precious ground.

For many summers I walk through concrete ways,
Where blackflies dance and dust blows like sand,
New homes and houses must be built they say,
But I have seen The Vanishing Land.

Nigel David Evans

A Gift To Ourselves

Hello, and what are you doing there?
I asked a child on a beach.
I'm burying my treasure, was the reply,
Keeping it out of reach,
So nobody can take it away from me.

Hello, and what are you doing there?
I asked a man in a field.
I am sowing seeds for a modified crop,
A good crop, with high yield,
So we will be able to feed crowds, you'll see.

Hello, and what are you doing there?
I asked workmen near a hole.
We are disposing of all unwanted waste,
Rejects from pole to pole.
The boy from the beach was like one of these men.

Hello, and what are you doing there?
I asked myself this one day
When I was standing in front of a coffin,
With folded hands to pray:
Dear Lord, please, take into Your care my love's soul.

The child's treasure was a plastic bag,
With a plastic cup and a toy.
Modified seeds, who knows, what we did to them,
Still meddling, man like boy.
Have we closed our minds to the damage we've done?

The plastic will not disintegrate,
Landfill-sides give in return
Back to us tenfold in poisonous gases.
Oft maiming the unborn.
And for all mankind, there is nowhere to run.

Helga I Dharmpaul

A PINCH OF HUMANITY

Chasing rainbows and shooting stars.
Can the echo warriors save Mars?
Our human nature craves affection,
while unleashed greed feeds aggression.

Cautious shadows below ripped skies,
give a glimpse of where the truth lies.
We are all too quick to point the finger of blame,
fork tongued as we hammer nails in the coffin of shame.

Cold stone hearts on icy thrones,
for trampled generations to atone
and reputations walk before us,
while we journey through life like on a bus.

Cover mankind with more than vanity
and get off your high horse of morality.
Wrestling with righteousness and ignorance.
Knowledge will always bleed some arrogance.

Chasing rainbows and shooting stars
with livid dreams in fast cars.
So take this pinch of humanity
and balance on the scales of sanity.

J R Griffiths

Our Environment

We committed a terrible crime against the planet earth.
Once it was beautiful and very healthy, but not any more since
God put us on it to enjoy forever.
What God had created was a wonderful world of beauty!
But we never understood His great creation.
We've done everything against God's will and we destroyed the very
important things that helped all of us to live and breath cleaner air!
For profit and for the progress we've destroyed ourselves.
Everybody who lives in the present, we have and we still do pollute
the environment.
In every way and place we go, we see there is a lot of rubbish -
in the land, in the river and in the sea.
The lovely sea was once the best and cleanest and very importantly,
it provided food for all of us.
Today it is no longer clean and we still eat the food from it,
and that is why we have committed a big crime.
We drink the water from the river and the sea, and the air we breath
is all polluted.
The environment cries for help for the damaged that we have all done
for years, but many people are still too greedy and they still pollute the
sea and the river and the air that we all breath.
I do say stop this crime and help our environment to make it better.

Antonio Martorelli

Trees

I believe trees have faces,
because I saw your gnarled features
profiled against a late evening sky
straining skyward;
pock-marked complexion
pitted by burning rain,
mouth open
exhaling life.

Your craggy face,
turned to faint frown,
by a warm gentle breeze,
new expression
echoing thoughts
of despair and disappointment,
in anticipation of
the destiny of your species.

Keith Coleman

DINNER TODAY

What shall we have for dinner today?
We hear frustrated mothers say
Something wholesome for our family
There's nothing safe . . . this is tragedy.

Chicken and eggs have salmonella
('Twas a good meal for a growing fella)
Now the cows too have the brain disease
This rules out other meals that please.

Sheep and lambs also carry that germ
Giving us all great cause for concern
Now sausages, chops and mince are out
Anything made with meat is in doubt.

The farmers were using tainted food
To feed the sows and all their brood
OK then let's have some fish for tea
But fish are poisoned in the sea.

We shall have to use the Soya bean
(A good substitute for that protein)
Are chemicals used to spray this crop?
Can it be too late for man to stop?

Valerie Ovais

NEMESIS

Where now the lark, who in my youth would make the sky resound?
Her bubbling notes cascading from on high.
Where can the droning bumblebee, or butterfly be found?
I ask the question with a passing sigh.

Departed, gone, unseen, unheard.
Like the bittern's echoing boom!

Where now the cowslip or forget-me-not, the harebell,
Or the meadow-sweet?
The scent of clover in the summer air, or tiny gentians,
Fragrant round our feet?

Gone, where we shall hear the final word,
Headlong, speeding to our doom!

All nature now it seems, is in our grasp,
To shape, or tailor to our needs,
But soon, man's follies will collapse,
In retribution for our selfish deeds!

Leonard Muscroft

PROBLEMS OF POLLUTION

Problems of pollution won't go away,
Problems of pollution are here to stay.

People, work hard to devise suitable plans,
Protect our lives and the future of 'man'.
Save the world from total devastation,
Left behind for later generations.
And let's work together, put wrongs right,
These problems won't just disappear from sight.

Susan Mullinger

DEATH OF THE BIRDS

I watched a flight of birds,
Packed at the earth.
Those poor birds didn't know,
They were courting an early death.
For the ground it had been sprayed,
By man with pesticides.
By man with his great love,
For the use on insecticides.

Poison to a little bird,
Other animals as well.
A warning is given to man,
But who the birds will tell?
Once men took great pride,
In the vegetables they grew.
Back then in those days,
Of pesticides they never knew.

Back then the birds flew free,
The air filled with their song.
Then came the age of technology,
Things changed before too long.
It's sad to say that man,
Is destroying our green earth.
To the creatures who share our world,
We bring them certain death.

M Muirhead

DOOMSDAY DOGGEREL

Acid rain is with us now
So is lead pollution
Ozone levels they are thin
What is the solution?
Man and beast, with flower and tree
All are thus affected
Planet Earth is poisoned too
Common-sense rejected.

Seas are thick with chemicals
Fishes they are gasping
Rivers run with gunge and filth
Will it be long-lasting?
Waste tips dumped with rubbish foul
Proof of Man's existence
Methane gas invades the soil
Where is our resistance?

Cancer levels they are high
So are pylons potent
Chernobyl its dust has spread
Barely took a moment.
Likewise oil fields in the Gulf
Set alight and burning
Petrol fumes invaded air
Time for some U-turning.

Greenpeace does its best to stir
Everybody's conscience
Men and nations look aside
Treating it as nonsense.
Friends of Earth are with them too
Working close together
We must heed them or lose out
From their bold endeavour.

Books abound like 'Silent Spring;
Issuing their warning
Man stays blinkered and hide-bound
Bored and but a-yawning
Children yet to come will find
World still sick and ailing
We their guardians all at fault
Heritage are failing.

Marion P Webb

Crimes Against The Planet

Us people, and I stress us all,
have plundered and raped this planet, till it is nearly beyond recall.
I think we as humans, have to shoulder the blame,
we must try hard to repair the damage, and see if it can be reclaimed.
We must replace our forests, we must plant more trees,
don't forget all the wildlife that lives in them, they are not there just
to please.
We have dug up so much of our natural resources, for fuel and power,
we should try other ways like, the wind or the waves, they'll not turn
things sour.
Compost our rubbish, cut down on waste,
eat more natural tings, though maybe not pretty that's no disgrace.
Why do we need nuclear power, another destructive force,
I'll never understand that, if I argue till I'm hoarse.
Oil spills in our seas, other pollutants in our rivers,
pesticides and preservatives on food, and all that delivers.
There are too many people, who will try anything to make a fortune,
they don't care about our planet, they show no caution.
Please God, let us be in time,
to put right our world, and stop the decline.

Ken Mills

A Hot Lethal Potion

When 'Satchmo' sang 'What a Wonderful World',
He expressed for mankind, that forgotten word
In praise of our planet - a jewel in space,
So taken for granted by the human race.
It stole the breath of the first men on the moon,
This beautiful orb in a blue-haze cocoon,
A ball of colour 'gainst a back-drop of night,
Compared to the lunar scene's drab ash grey light.
Their lives changed forever, so humbled in awe,
This really was 'Eden' - a world to adore.

The natural beauty of earth is unique,
- The emerald green sea, and white bays of Mustique,
Sahara's great dunes ever changing their shape,
The vast Table Mountain of Africa's Cape,
The satanic dark waters of Norway's' fjords,
And Switzerland's Alps with such scenic rewards.
The Great Barrier Reef, with its myriads of fish,
All rainbow colours, like an art deco dish.
The harsh 'ice-age' landscape of Antarctic's freeze,
Where winds howl and shriek, like a Dervish on skis,
And the world's great problems are nothing but dreams,
When life, means surviving climatic extremes.

So, what of this world, we so shamefully abuse,
Where only large oil spills can make the world news,
And unscrupulous tippers conceal toxic waste,
While chainsaws eat forests, which are never replaced,
And nuclear waste is dumped in the ocean?
- Our gift to the future - a hot lethal potion.

O R Hounsell

My Senses

Are you ready for this now
Is your mind and body true,
Are you ready for this now
Have you thought it clearly through?

Do you see the things I see
Sudden visions from the past,
Do you see the things I see
Reformations birth at last?

Do you hear the sounds I hear
Of migrant souls screaming loud,
Do you hear the sounds I hear
Of soft voices in the crowd?

Do you feel the way I feel
The hounding need of lost repose,
Do you feel the way I feel
Earth's abusers now to loath?

Do you touch the things I touch
Searching softly through your eyes,
Do you touch the things I touch
Tactile life that passes by?

Please love the things I love
Of compassion and respect,
Please love the things I love
Longing, patience and regret?

Please love the things I love
Of forgiveness and surprise,
Please love the things I love
For only then the earth shall rise.

Sally Colgate

Deep Secrets

So many secrets
'neath your opaque operculum
a thousand years
a million
much more
infinite, eternal
You've claimed lives
hearts, souls
Your power so great
cannot be fought
cannot be captured

Cities beneath
Atlantis
and others
wrecks with treasures
gold,
sparkling jewels
now hiding places for crustaceans,
marine life
anchors for barnacles

Man's endless quest
to conquer
You will not submit
not reveal
only snippets
of your wealth
gas,
oil
in return we pollute
poison

Your boundless might
cannot be harnessed
many try
many lose
We rob you
we pay the price
always you win
So deep
man cannot survive
Your secrets safe forever

Elizabeth Walker

SEPARATRIX STROKE OBLIQUE STROKE SEPARATRIX

Esteemed remorseful professors
Having become the dark destroyers
Solidus also separatrix separatrix
Numerator from denominator
Atoning light
Sparking atomic weights
And mass into energy
Having known the seasons propinquity and
Sipping thin tea through tight lips
In the cemeteries of the closed mind
The ultimate reasons violating and
Sitting around in cycle clips
Within the confines of space time
The autumnal leaves turning and burning, on
Equinox and solstice dates
At either point of the ecliptic
While Cancer and Capricorn waits
The changing volatility
Of brown earth turning and burning
Turning and burning, turning and burning.

James Colton

One World

Today there is no love
And how many tomorrows must pass
Before I feel its reassuring touch.

Today there is no pain
But how long before love bleeds
Its sorrow from my heart.

Today there is no hope
All optimism retained by that past
Which holds my loneliness captive.

Today there is no freedom
As I pace this cage of life
Which holds my soul.

Today there is no peace
And no one knows my grief
As the discord of the world reigns.

Today I hear tomorrow calling
And wish only for a time
When my troubles blend to obscurity
Against the background of this pitied world.

Paula Hind

The Killing Of Mother Earth

Progress they called it when they invented the car,
Now choking the earth, an invisible scar.
Poisoning our children and killing with speed,
No longer a luxury, everyone's greed.

The disposable nappy, every parent's dream.
Now buried in millions, the earth gives a scream.
Making life easier would seem to have a price,
But is the convenience worth the sacrifice?

We create life in a test-tube, childless couples rejoice.
Embryos frozen, potential life, but who gives them a voice?
A moral dilemma, so who has the right, to say what should be so?
Mother Nature helpless to save, gave up long ago.

So gaze long at all of life's beauty, remember it while it's still there,
The species extinct, never retrieved, should have made us care.
The clues are all around us, we see them every day,
Therefore, when we've destroyed it all, don't ask what part you played.

Beverley Christian

CRIME AGAINST THE PLANET

Life can be so lonely
Life can be so sad
We feel we are in a wilderness
Children are not born bad
Do people have to argue?
Do they really have to fight?
Don't they know how precious time is
That is doesn't matter who is right?
The wasted years or worry
The time that's so ill spent
Why wait until it's too late
Before we should repent.
Each day our thoughts behind us
Remembering past events
Or wishing for the future
To hold happier achievements
We really must try harder
To accept things day by day
Enjoy the gift of life itself
For dead we *'never may'*.

Joan Patrickson

Paradise Ignored

You've let us loose in your front room of treasures
All you so carefully crafted we stumbly blindly into
We don't care what we destroy
Most of the time we don't even notice.

You planned, designed, moulded and loved into being
And we use and abuse without a thought
Even each other, your masterpieces, we do not value
Worst of all we have no sense of loss.

You must want so much for us
Your motivation was purely love
How your heart must bleed we cannot comprehend
Perhaps it is better that we do not know.

You know the end from the beginning
I wonder why, when you knew what we would do
You still gave us the chance
It's too late now for going back.

Do you regret it all?
Even in your omniscience were you prepared?
Prepared for the depths of our perversion
And the pain that we must surely cause you?

I hope that the moments when we stop
When we are reduced to silence at some aspect of you
And between sins, say we are sorry
That we can somehow make up for what we do.

Joanne Maden

Ps And Qs Plead For Peace And Quality

Preach to the producers of CFCs that
puncture the ozone, a parallel to pouring
petrol over us then lighting a pyre,
and quench the pyromaniacs.

Pulverise the pulpers of forests and
plead with the people who permit pollution
to pass through sewers and pipes,
and persuade them to quit.

Prevent the population from propagating
to plague proportions, and the punitive
use of plutonium power for arms,
and so protect perpetuation.

Question the producers of pesticides
which prodigiously poison plants and
then prevaricate on their pathogeny,
and quell their practices.

Query persons who procrastinate while
pollution proliferates and perpetrate
pathological policies, in politics,
and positions of power.

Quiescent or quelled into quitting their
quota of pressure, let no one be, lest
our planet be propelled into a painful
and premature passing.

Dot Martin

FOXES OF THE FUTURE

Coughing,
he closes the newspaper,
bored of reading of the worldwide epidemic
of cancer killing hundreds
of millions of people.

Through his kitchen window,
he sees two foxes emerge
from the backyard bushes.
He grabs his rifle and rushes outside.
Two shots, two foxes lay dead.

'Why did you kill them, Daddy?
Foxes are nearly extinct.'

'I know they're almost extinct.
That's why I killed them.
And when they are extinct,
their skins will be worth a fortune!'

A hundred million miles away,
an armed fleet of alien starships
flies in a straight line
towards earth.

David Rhine

WHAT IS MAN?

The silver gull-grey aeroplane
has ripped the perfect pale blue sky apart;
and through the rift
the frothy clouds spill out,
bubbling in its wake
from the bright white layer beyond;
the gap widening as I watch.

Man - the expert -
Mother Nature's enemy -
destroyer and despoiler of the earth,
reaches up to rape the Heavens above us.
If no more predators disturb the peace
the rift may heal.

John S Mercer

THE LIFE WITHIN

Take a deep breath,
how does it feel?
Enjoy it while you can,
'cause soon enough,
they'll be no air,
left for us to breathe.

Every can that you spray,
takes your breath away.
Every tree that gets cut down,
is killing us day by day.

So as you walk
by lakes and streams,
and say 'What pretty colours,'
those pretty colours,
- oil on water,
will kill the life within.

So stop right now,
and take a look,
at how you live your life,
do you play your own part,
in the destruction of our planet?

Claire O'Connor

Lost For Evermore

Red shiny coke can nestled in the long meadow grass
White shiny plastic bags caught up in the hedgerows
Silver shiny supermarket trolley marooned in the canal
Myriads of empty bins with 'litter' written on them
Fag end pavements, graffiti covered walls
Distressed, dog messed, throw away world
Your snazzy sunnies miss the blueness
Of the sky, and your personal stereo ears
Blast birds

Oblivious to the human filth
That's poured into the sea
You don your designer wetsuit
And take to the water ski
So you can't hear the dolphins crying
'Please, please, let us be'

Those human words
Float on the tide of consumables
But never reach the shore
Because blocked by the drifting debris
They are lost for evermore.

B King

Questions!

Why do we kill and wound and maim?
What is the point of all this war?
What do we feel we have to gain?
Do we really know what it's all for?

Why can't man live side by side
And heal this Earth through love and peace?
Love his neighbour and be his guide
Instead of hounding him for his different beliefs?

Does it matter if we are black, yellow brown or white
Catholic, Buddhist, Jew or Christian?
Why is it we never see the light.
And seek to hasten our own destruction?

We see miracles on our planet at every turn.
The changing seasons, the miracle of birth.
But there is one miracle that only we can work.
It's so simple - cease the fighting and unite the Earth . . .

Linda M Crook

OUR LEGACY

Mass production, consumer demand
It's killing the planet
And poisoning the land
Rubbish dumps full
Of plastic and tin
Cars, washers, fridges
It's a sin
The ozone is turning
Into a big black hole
Entering into it
Is our soul.

Our survival depends
On the air we breathe
To the next generation
This planet we'll leave
If we carry on poisoning
The soil and the sea
Not much of a legacy
Will there be.

Brenda Reville

THE LEGACY

Bigger, better, faster,
We had the best intentions.
There was going to be world peace,
It was the greatest of inventions.

We opened our Pandora's box,
Unleashed its terrible power,
Split a tiny little atom,
Saw it drop its deadly shower.

We sought to quell the mouths to feed
With a simple little pill,
We conquered Mother Nature
And thought we'd gained free will!

Little knowing what it meant,
Little knowing what would come,
We were much too close,
To see what we had done.

The people still are suffering,
War, famine and the rest,
In a world that's growing smaller,
Well, at least we did our best.

You can see deforestation,
And pollution in the sea,
It's the hidden, lurking dangers
Should worry you and me.

For every good beginning,
There can be a sticky end,
So choose your path wisely
And be brave, so brave, my friend.

S Duff

PROTEST?

Education is beneficial,
Technology a good thing,
The planet sacrificial,
When Mammon is king.

Conferences and debates
Are held on global warming,
But none of this relates
To vices habit forming.

So we leave all the lights on,
Put out bin bags by the score,
Shop in hypermarkets,
And not the local store.

The government decries the waste
Of our natural resources,
But U-turns in haste
When equipping the Armed Forces.

Programmes are made on deforestation
And soil loss when it rains,
While global corporations
Pour chemicals down the drains.

The individual can campaign
For planetary betterment,
But will voices in suburbia
Sway our apathetic government?

Abi Preston

The Legacy

Once, I stood in beauty here,
With needles bright each spring.
My branches hung like graceful skirts
And I enjoyed the rain.
I saw my clear reflection
In the sparkling lake below,
And other trees would sway with me
Dancing as the wind sang low.
The forest then was proud and full
Of every kind of life,
But now the water at my feet
Poisons all in view:
No fish, no plants, just creeping slime
As death keeps pouring down.
My branches have no needles now,
They look like shrivelled bones,
And bark lies leprous on the ground
Devoid of any green;
And this once glorious hillside
Is seared as in a fire.
As acid fills our burning pores
We die a lingering death,
And wonder when this killing field
Will be avenged.

Jane Ward

AND GOD CREATED MAN

In the beginning, it has been said,
God, made the earth and it was good.
All creatures great and small, He made,
and gave to them, what grew, for food.
Then God brought out His master plan,
took up some clay and modelled man.
A woman next, was brought to life,
and Eve became a model wife.
God took His creatures by the hand,
and led them to a Promised Land.
'Now listen well,' He said to them,
'This place is yours, and it's known as Eden.
I give it to you, for your joy and pleasure,
to work and to play in, to tend and to treasure.
But remember my children, with others you dwell,
respect your companion and treat them well.
Then off God went and left those two,
who multiplied without further ado.
- Several thousand years on, and few floods later,
how did man repay his creator?
He waged war on others, invented the gun,
he shot at God's creatures, he killed them for fun.
He plundered the seas and the forests he burned,
'Progress,' said man, 'How much we have learned!'
But God and His angels wept at man's greed,
and God said 'I wish to God, I hadn't invented this breed.'

Kym Best

DEATH OF A PLANET

Sometimes I look out of my window and wonder why
seeing what was once beautiful, at human hands, begins to die

What was given by divine spirit as a gift for us all to cherish
now before me through human intervention begins to perish

Something has to be done to make people see before it is too late
or they will carry on blindly destroying our planet, death will be its fate

Looking around watching what was once there and was once here
realising that all the beauty I had once known was now beginning
to disappear

One day what I once knew will be gone forever, it will be out of sight
do the people doing this know they are wrong and must know it is
not right?

Please do not destroy this beautiful planet earth?
it is here for us all, it is our world, the place of our birth

Looking around in disbelief and total disarray
seeing nature turn rotten and begin tó decay

I have been informed about the slow but sure death of the ozone layer
I sit and contemplate and know that the people doing this cannot
really care

If these people are not prevented from what they are doing one day
then what we once had will be no more, it will die and go away

There are scientists who do not always realise what they are doing until
it is too late, these are the people who without realising play around
with other people's fate

So to you all I say, stop and think what you are doing and simply say
this, do not give this planet the ultimate death kiss

Wally

The Killing Of Cwm-Iscoed

Cwm-Iscoed - fields of shimmering green,
An endlessly changing verdant sheen.
Valley sides, once rich with trees
That shivered in the upland breeze.

A rippling stream in loud delight
Proclaimed its undisputed right
To wind through meadows, woods and hedgerows.
To shelter flashing trout and minnows.

Along the moorland paths raised high
Against the deep-blue, cloudless sky,
Long lines of snow-white, woolly sheep
Flocked to the plains down scarpments steep.
Behind them drovers, lilting as they spoke
In a tongue unknown to lowland folk.

But then, the hands of greedy men
Laid waste the beauty of this glen.
Ripping the earth for coal and ore,
Stripping the hillside, scarring the moor.
Thrusting long arms of sterile shale
Along the fertile, verdant vale.

White flocks no longer bedeck the green,
Tho' some tattered remnants, grey and lean,
Eke out a life, uncherished, bland.
Raiders in their own homeland.

Cwm-Iscoed's Life gave way to Wealth,
Yet two things survived as though by stealth.
The Tongue, the shepherd's pride;
The Tongue by which they lived and died.
And the Songs they sang, in grief or joy.
These two no change will ever destroy.

Chris Hassell

Crimes Against The Planet And Ourselves

(From Rev. 11:18b)

Men of greed, scientists, and fools,
With hearts of stone,
Search for wealth and academic glories,
Cause sufferings reaching the human bone.

All life on earth, and our air, they're
Allowed to selfishly spoil,
With a million contaminants against
Every child's future life and toil.

But the Alpha and Omega through John, and
In anger did prophetically say:
of, 'the time to destroy those who destroy
the earth.' - Although destroying it still today.

His advanced warnings were given, to those
Pumping earth's black blood from below;
From steel-like copses in the sea. They were
Burned. Yet the defiance of others still show.

Decommissioning nuclear plants, scientists fear,
And with excuses, cowardly delay;
Perhaps until they've lived their lives on earth,
And conveniently pass away.

Esdras was told of days when, 'women will give
Birth to monsters'. Lord, clonings has begun!
Surely Lord, wickedness is now full grown?
While we patiently await the arrival of Your Son.

Yet we pollute with our cars, because we're too
Many, and we hate doing without a single thing;
We're fatter than ever, putting too much sugar,
Salts, and fats in our food, in just about everything.

R Thomas

Twentieth Century Guilt

As the twenty-first century approaches
Earth's citizens look back in horror.
Two world wars caused death and deprivation.
There were murders, rapes, theft and arson.
Decent people recoil at the constant misery
and fear brought about by other's greed.

Our children are brought up to swear.
They demand designer clothes and shoes.
They're rude to their parents and elders.
They argue and shout at their friends.
They bully younger and weaker classmates
smiling in ecstasy as their victims bleed.

Our animals are tortured continually
by scientists and factory farmers,
by hunters with rods or guns and dogs,
by cruel owners who beat and starve them,
often tying them up for days on end
without taking care of their needs.

We've exploded bombs in our atmosphere
and burnt great holes in the ozone layer.
We spray dangerous pesticides on our crops,
we make furniture out of poisonous materials
which burst into flames so we can't breathe.
We appear to thrive on miserable deeds.

Let's hope the next century will be better
and we'll finally learn to love our neighbours
whether black, white, red or yellow.
Allow them to worship any way they choose
and give them the freedom of their karma.
Listen to the wisdom man and take heed.

Daf Richards

EXPLORING OUTER SPACE

The Lord did create, Earth, land and sea
But inventors created things like electricity
The telephone, the telly and much much more
Made the life of mankind, much easier to bear
Not satisfied with these, they landed on the moon
They sent further spaceships
To further peruse and walk in outer space
Millions and millions of money spent
Mission accomplished, whatever next?
Why interfere with the natural world?
Why let people starve and children die
From want of medication
Concord for speed, aircraft mishaps
Thousands of lives lost in the sky
Look at the people that have died
Open a cock-pit and see modern techniques
The wrong button pressed and trouble does start
Computers are ruining everything
Even the world stands in danger
Of modern techniques
One press of a button by mistake
Or in haste
What happens next?

Sheila Wall

FOOL'S GOLD YELLOW

Fool's gold-yellow, pillar-box red,
some colours of man, stuck in our heads,
light sky-blue, deep sea-green,
colours of nature our minds rarely see.

The fresh colours of nature, the dark shades of man,
we seem to prefer the latter, but I don't understand.
The sea and sky are natural, as are plants and trees.
Nature didn't invent the brick, that's a mistake by you and me.
So let's give up trying to copy the natural tones,
let all the wildlife be, and just leave nature alone.

Raymond Mandeville

OUR EARTH

Man's greed for finite sources
disregards long term effects,
as we suppress the voice of reason,
and stifle warning checks.

Man has struggled with imbalance
within the natural world,
but even short term vision
now sees this blight unfurled.

We create a false illusion
with each new challenge faced,
of an aura of advancement
clouding inexorable waste.

Once at one with nature
now we squander what was gain,
and as we languish in modernity
our star begins to wane:

Cheated by pollution
erasing value from the earth;
a land that man leaves lifeless,
extracting all that it was worth.

Susan Turner

It Is Time I Spoke

It's time I spoke
although it may be too late
you have ignored me for far too long
yet it is I who gives you food
it is I who provides you with the air that you breathe
without me you would not exist
yet you tear me apart
you have raped me repeatedly
and will do so again
you have torn out my insides
you have polluted me
you scatter your waste
and use everything for your own greedy well-being
you have turned my tears to acid
you are close to making me barren
life is not short
I have been here longer than you
but my future is now unsure
listen to what I say
before it's too late

Gabby Copperstone

The World Today

The world was meant to be a place
Of love, for all the human race
To live in perfect harmony,
And share the fruits of land and sea.

But we have lost the will to share
With those who have no-one to care,
And greed and envy, power and hate,
Are standards set to motivate.

The world is now a sorry place
Of suffering for the human race.
There's hunger, strife, and constant war,
So many rich, too many poor.

If we don't learn to live and share
Our love with people everywhere,
We'll all become the helpless poor,
And lose the world for evermore.

Derek Richings

PLANET SWEET

I'd like to offer up a prayer
For a disappearing ozone layer
Let us spray.
The million little things that died
Covered in insecticide,
The blackened leaves that curl in pain
Bowing down to acid rain,
The cars that billow out their fumes
The strangled air in smoke-filled rooms
The toxic waste that's oozing in
Starving rivers of oxygen.
The concrete wastelands we create
So market men can speculate,
The forests felled so they can feed
A short-lived wealth and long-term greed.
The creeping drought in man-made dust.
We close our eyes and ears and just
Say 'Let us spray.'

Russell Adams

HOPE?

Why did God create the destructive animal man?
I gaze in wonder at clouds
and in their changing patterns
I can see the world changing
from pristine innocence to sad degradation.
Time was when rivers ran clean,
fields fertilised naturally,
woods managed sympathetically
in ways helpful to mankind.
In a misguided way he thought he knew better,
Nature's way disregarded, chemicals were kings.
The path downhill commenced, Earth's beauty desecrated.
Now he has started thinking
how to repair the damage
to his mother, Planet Earth
with regret and repentance.
Maybe - just maybe, there is hope for mankind yet!

Ivy Allpress

CRIMES AGAINST THE PLANET

The planet Earth has been here for millions of years,
Balance between all that lived, lived upon it was once correct,
But then man came along and started to destroy the balance by
Committing terrible crimes.
They started to steel from everyone and ended up in jail,
Steeling from everyone affected us all by knowing not what to do
Or where to hide our properties,
And driving their cars over speed limit, affected us by running
Someone over.
The lovely view and scenery has been spoilt with litter all over,
When will people stop crimes against the planet Earth?

Fatima Jamshad (16)

MOTHER EARTH

In my subliminal awareness I see before me a living, moving earth
I hear its heart as an unborn child
I smell its milken breast
I lay upon its lap and I am comforted
I love my Mother Earth she speaks to me in the silence of thought
She is beautiful but my heart aches for her, for she is dying
Her children raped her, drained her, tore her apart
They broke her heart
They broke her strong back
They starved her of love and filled her body with poisons
They worked her and dredged her until she swooned faded and aged
Now her children born of feet and wing hunger and thirst and curse her
As an unfruitful fig tree struck by lightning
Her children are merciless
They dig into her bowels and drain her marrow
Her waters of tears are dried
Her array of seasons, time is no more
She suffered long with her loving and giving
Her balance has gone awry
Oh what will you do without me is her sigh
Soon! Soon! I will take back all my babes within my bowels when
I die.
Because I am their life they suckled me too much
They gave me nought a mother's burden is too much to bear
When her children forget to care
Oh my babes!
My demise is your despair.

Agnes Burns Lawson

Mother Nature Dreams In Whispers

I wanted to dream
You wouldn't let me sleep
I wanted to dream of flowers
To dream of trees
Whales diving in the sea
Dolphins singing to the wind
My soul surfing in a colourful swirl to the end
of the earth and back again
But the world is dying
And nobody is crying
Acid rain is burning the globe with sorrow
With bitter pain the silent squeal of countless trees
Pierces the sky as they are cut down
Lifeless limbs to wasteful tastes of greed
It seems nearly too late to mend
Is the world coming to an end?
It's like a kind of fate we created for ourselves
We're all to blame
Yet fingers point at each other
The answer is in the sky
An explosion of gloom covers the land
The sea is turning into mud
As the landscape becomes a map of uninhabitability
I want to sleep
You won't let me sleep
Dying world
Human greed is destroying your need to breathe
I wanted to dream the earth was well
A beautiful place to live
Now in a state of sickness and soon to be a dwelling hell.

L Lucas

INHUMANITY

The dodo and the mammoth, the pterodactyl too,
No longer live upon the Earth beside both me and you.
They are extinct because of man - the havoc that they reap.
And this will also happen to the mammals of the deep!
The seal is one such species, so harmless you'll agree
They bask in sun on beaches - and swim inside our sea.
But this is now polluted, something they cannot feel
And it is now destroying this harmless little seal.
They do not ask for much from life - just somewhere safe to stay.
To swim and fish, to breed with ease and sometimes even play!
But men will go out culling, to strip them of their skin
For humans to wear this coat and keep them warm within,
As if this wasn't bad enough - the seas must be made safer
From this cause however long - we must never waiver.
Without the help of humans the seal will surely perish.
And this once lovely creature will not be there to cherish.
The dreadful death they now face, we cannot comprehend
Their natural home which gives them life, will soon bring forth their end!
With little ones born diseased, parents dying daily,
Plaintive cries sound everywhere, no food to feed their baby.
We cannot let this happen! And just stand idly by
Watching as without our help the seal will fade and die.
And years from now when all that's left are pictures on a page,
It will be much too late for man to fly into a rage
And scream and shout and publicise the things we should alter
To make it safe for such as these to live within the water
Now is the time for action! To make rules that last,
So that the seal can stay for good - and not be in the past!

Letitia Snow

DEATH FOR THE COUNTRYSIDE

Looking over the countryside,
Hills enveloped in mist,
It all looks so peaceful,
Until the JCB thunders past.

The yellow monster
Moves slowly, elegantly,
Destroying all in its wake

And its place,
Where there was destruction,
A building now grows.

Vitality for man,
Death for the countryside.

Adrian Procter

TOO LATE

Did you notice how the trees today
Do not welcome rain in the normal way
Curled up leaves just fall away
As acid rain is here to stay.

Slugs that devastate my plants
Won't even get another chance
Blue pellets that they rush to eat
Has put them to eternal sleep.

How much more do we need to end
Before we say it's time to mend
For all the damage that's been done
I think it's all too late, my son.

Roland G Powell

A Woodland Walk

Seldom, have I walked along this lonely way,
keeping to the path, in the hope not to stray,
light cascading, through the forest above
simulating shadows, like a puppet on a glove.

Being alone, but for man's best friend,
we followed the trail, right to the end.
Passing streams of crystal clear
water-culminating through its weir.

Sights and sounds, exciting and new,
heightened by the morning dew,
singing birds, echo the morn,
heralding another summer dawn.

Our last steps are taken, with grass at our feet
the causeway approaching, tarmac, concrete,
the sound of the cars, their engines playing tunes
as they thunder along, emitting their fumes!

Surely to God! if we only took time
to stroll - with one's dog through the countryside
we'd realise that nature, is a wonderful friend
it would be such a shame, if it all came to an end!

Brian Waterhouse

Planet Earth To Man

Extinction is forever,
Means never coming back
And if man isn't careful,
The Earth may answer back.
Extinction is forever,
Man's never coming back.

Cilla Pocklington

The Rape Of A Dale

they come with hooves and with wheels
(the prey have no accessories as these)
they park their cars in rows on grass
the owners stand and look through glass
they think we understand, us rural folk
they imagine we comply not provoke
an argument against the hue and cry
of whether a fox should live or die
the pleasure gained of those on hoof
does not really amount to proof
that foxes are a pest and so must die
(imagine if that to you or I apply)
the fox is not a culinary dish
although he too needs his pound of flesh
he is a fellow resident in the dale
why do they place him beyond the pale
how can I defend his pleasure
how can I atone their leisure
if only they could let creatures be
and perceive they are the same as you and me
we don't seem able to shift their perspective
so to the fox we will be protective
direct action is what we have left
or else from our conscience we will be bereft
salute our champions in action in prison or dead
there has been enough talking and enough has been said

Margaret Graham

Get Wise

We need the trees, we need the flowers
We need the plants - their healing powers
We need the seas with no pollution
We need the ice-caps, we need a solution
M is for murderer, M is for man
His own greatest enemy, destroying the land . . .
. . . Air pollution, nuclear waste
Garbage dumped and left in haste
Toxins in every drop of water
Acid raining as the world gets hotter
And who cares about the deforestation?
The loss of tribes and the whole of their nation
Species of animals become extinct
But humans never stop and think
Just bulldoze ahead and rip everything down
Ignore the global warming going around
Keep burning the fossil fuels, produce CO_2
The world's an oyster - but the pearls are few
The greenhouse effects not just for plants
Ozone depletion not just a chance
These problems won't just disappear
And, maybe, we should all now live in fear
Mother Earth is dying from mismanagement of our ways
Can this damage be rectified, or have we numbered our days?
We are all interdependent, every man and beast
But within this intricate web of life our precious planet weeps
We're killing her slowly and the day she dies
Man will go with her, so don't blow it - *get wise.*

W Carlin

One World

One world we have
There is no spare
The damage that's caused
Will be hard to repair

With oil spills
And nuclear waste
Rainforests are disappearing
At an alarming pace

The hole in the ozone
Is increasing in size
Will its total destruction
Be the ultimate prize

What will be left
For the generations to come
Will they be living in darkness
To hide from the sun

John Evans

I Tried

I will live my life,
Till all possibilities have gone,
I shall learn from nature,
For what my life beholds.
Then let it be said I tried,
For if I die today, or tomorrow,
Then I shall reach the heavenly tide.

Jemma Howard (14)

UNTITLED

Our planet Earth has not a dearth of growth or food,
It's our quest to use its products,
We're ill-mannered and rude, abusing it thoughtlessly,
But there's plenty for all, though we often ignore
Mother Nature's and God's call,
Not appreciating our Earth's wonder and bounty.
It serves us right to suffer the misery we bring
By committing decimation against people and things.
In decimating rainforests for wood,
To the ugly and beautiful creatures' habitats
This is certainly never good.
Loss of habitat can cause creatures' extinction.
However can we do this when God creates everything
For man and woman, girl and boy, and the joy it will bring.
So then comes conservation to preserve this thing,
Of wonderful creation, fascination and a ring
Of never-ending learning about science,
And other kinds of learning too.
So our minds can have daily joy anew.
Brings back some lost joy in preserving
Many a herd of animals or of birds
God created so lovingly for our joy,
To fascinate, inspire and cheer us,
Every man, woman, girl and boy.

Jean H Davy

Making Inroads

M idst the rubble, filth, destruction
O f a land that once had mattered,
T ossed aside, the dreams of many
O rdered lives lie torn and shattered.
R uined (by the Unconcerned armed
W ith marauding beasts of prey)
A re the lives of Innocents whose
Y esterdays are swept away . . .

B oring ceaselessly through Earth where
U nscathed beauty once had been;
I n a frenzy, oust the people.
L ife no matter, (just machine!)
D oomed to hopelessness, new-homeless
I n sad eyes, with tears empearled.
N o love spare them - Devil take them!
G o by car - *pollute the world* -

Susan Devlin

Greenpeace

G enuine people who care for this world
R esources dwindling - it's really absurd
E ndangered species that's what we will be
E nvironment ravaged, we take all we see
N ext generation, how will they cope
P ollution clinging makes everything choke
E arth could be dying but what can we do
A ll work together the difference is you
C ompanies and government bleeding us dry
E volution means we get just one try

John Sarginson

TIME TO CARE

Man is held responsible for life's progress so it's said.
He's used the brains developed within his human head.
His ego grown, his pride became to mean all things to him
Did he not see where it would lead or were his eyes too dim.

The world was once a place of beauty, pure and airified
What's happened with pollution, now that purity has died.
The air is full of toxins which destroy the ozone layer,
How can we stop this madness? Should we offer up a prayer.

Are we to be destroyed as well by heat we cannot bear
Or will we drown in flooded rivers caused by rain out there.
Tornadoes, tidal waves as well with rising seas we'll see,
Is this the way our world will end and we will cease to be.

We did not see how nature worked to balance life on earth
Oh no, the pride of man must show what cleverness is worth.
The easy life he hankered for is not so very clever now
For danger it has put us in, can we escape somehow?

The crimes we have committed against this world of ours
Seem to be quite senseless when we think of shady bowers
Where healthy trees stood graciously without a thought of pain
Which would cause them to be dying from effects of acid rain.

Does mankind regret the progress when they're counting up the cost,
Do they realise what they've done and what we all have lost?
We just hope their wondrous brains can prove that they can
    now reverse
The havoc they have caused to all within the universe.

Frieda Cox

You Vs The World

It is important to know who started this,
As important as knowing who your parents *were*.
Do you like to be comfortable, warm, fed?
How about a nice garden, you know you like your bed.
The car, how many valves?
The sofa . . . oh, yeah . . .
I'm gonna get one with my bonus this month.
Have you read J Hawkes' latest?
Ikea this evening, then we'll go on the piss.
Did you think anymore about this . . .
Men and women?
Business studies?
How to cope with stress?
Death?
Health?
Wealth?
Wealth? Yes . . . of course you have.
Keep yearning, don't stop earning,
you haven't got many years left.

John Guilor

This Earth . . .

This wondrous earth - beyond all comprehension!
Such power and beauty, all part of God's plan.
Throughout the years a thirst and search for knowledge
Has drawn the energies of man
We honour all the vast achievements
We stand in awe at mankind's latest quest
Yet in the midst of modern daily living
We take the risk of losing what is best.

The countryside, so full of living wonder
The fields and rivers, coast and sea and sky
Are suffering from our careless lack of forethought,
Pollution causing precious things to die
We must take steps to halt this sad destruction
Not give it cause to escalate
Be careful of our great resources
And do it now, before it is too late!

Margaret E Dowson

Heavenly Observation!

In outer space for us is a feeling uncomplimentary, as other intelligent beings, have for centuries us been seeing, I think they must be celebrating, as from us, they continue to keep isolating, in fact, as we use science to attempt them to contact, all our efforts they will counteract!
For mankind that inherited this Earth, are not motivated, by need, instead, Earthlings are inspired by greed, for we dig out of the bowels of the Earth, minerals and indeed anything of worth, we don't even avoid. Busy with this employment, reducing the size of the Earth's girth, we break all the rules, we ignorant fools, changing our oceans and seas into cesspools, our own atmosphere we injure, year after year, nobody stole it, we made the hole in it, yet we continue the facts to ignore, as man with each other is eternally, it seems, to be at war.
Yes our observers must find, that Earthling, is someone to deplore.
Content to keep the resolution, that with continued pollution, our Earth will soon be no more . . .
Surely with our anti-natural crime, there will come the time, when all must atone for this crime. Could it even be very soon, as we fly our pleasure trip up to the moon?
Will our universe suddenly reverse, leaving us one and all, completely marooned?

B H Howell

THIS PLANET WE CALL HOME

The world is dying there's fear and there's dread
If man doesn't do something, then it soon will be dead.
The children are crying, 'There's nowhere to go'
What of the future, they just don't know.

There's fighting and dying, but few seem to care
People must see, they must be made aware
Of the damage to this planet, we call home
This constant demolition we cannot condone.

We've cut down the forest, wildlife had been lost
Man is so selfish he doesn't count the cost.
Nature battles to compensate, let's give her a break
How much more devastation can this world take.

Horrific evil weapons pit man against man
I'm sure this wasn't part of nature's great plan.
Man needs to analyse, try to understand
What is needed to save this; Our Land.

We should all join together in one united voice
Shout the world over 'We have the choice'.
Let's throw away the weapons, be free of hunger and pain
And let nature once more her balance regain.

Clean up the planet let it be pollution free
Make it a better world for our children to be.

Iris Taylor

ELEGY FOR THE COUNTRYSIDE

Golden-yellow fields of corn
Unfolding to distant horizons;
Lush pastures of emerald green
Caressed by crystal streams.

Meadows ablaze with buttercups,
Ox-eyed daisies and cowslips;
Hills and dales aflame with oats,
Blending with wheaten valleys.

Vales of kaleidoscopic colour;
Chessboard leas unrolling
To where a factory chimney smokes.

Verdant grasses wither and pale
Before a nuclear power station.

Chemical streams sizzle and hiss,
Fizz and pop with pollution.

Rivers curl with contamination.

Oil slicks spread round coasts and shores.

Ooze creeps along beaches; seas congeal.

Oceans freeze.

Robert D Hayward

STOP CHOPPING

Stop chopping down all those trees
Please, please hear my plea
Far too much land now we can see
On where they used to stand as they gave us a helping hand
To breathe.

Stop chopping down all those trees
You should see that you are hurting all those people as well as me
Just so you can make a few paper cups
Is it really good enough.

Stop chopping down all those trees
Just please, please hear my plea
For the children of tomorrow
Will need some air to breathe.

Keith L Powell

WHY!

'Grandfather why can't I walk on the grass?'
'Because your grandmother did when she was a lass.'
'Grandfather why can't I pick the flowers?'
'Because your grandmother did to pass her hours.'
'Grandfather tell me about the snow!'
'That was something we got a long time ago.'
'Grandfather why can't I touch a tree?'
'Maybe one day - just wait and see.'
'Grandfather did the people not care?'
'Yes, but to Mother Nature they didn't play fair.'
'Grandfather will our planet get strong?'
'Yes, when we put right what we got wrong.'
'Grandfather where is grandmother now?'
'In heaven my darling, still wondering how!'

Marilyn Porritt

Hi Sonny, Come Here And Read This

There are so many crimes on our planet,
Would not, you say so Janet?
There is the breaking of car windows,
Which means, the owner has to buy new windows.
The breaking of gravestones,
How would you like it, if when you die, it happens to your tomb?
There's the breaking of windows in empty houses,
Do you realise you are making it cold for the rats and mice?
Putting obstructions on a railway track
Could cause a serious crash at that.
Do not play on railway lines,
As you could end up dead, some time.
Taking things out of other people's houses,
A good job you did not meet the spouses.
Speeding on the public highway
Only takes one slip-up, and you can be dead that day.
Why, why, why rape a female; well,
Get yourself a girlfriend instead of heading for a prison cell.
Riding your bike on the pavement and knocking the elderly over,
How would you like it, if a car came along and knocked you
into a field of clover,
Getting your friend drunk and taking his money,
That is a very bad idea, Sonny.
Breaking up young trees, which are for years to come a must,
Do you realise when grown up will keep wind and rain off us?
Why sit in a car and get too fat,
Start waking and you will become as fit as a cat.
The air is getting thinner each day,
So should the cars on this Earth still stay?
Whatever you do be happy on your way,
When both of you are in love, you will make hay.

Ernest Maynard Thompson

WILL IT NEVER END?

Pollution punish our sadistic lives
With evil-smelling pesticides
Rapid vapours of chemical waste
Edging nearer to our homes at alarming haste

Stop wasting time on fanatic capers
Making hay whilst your wicked vipers
Penetrate the Earth's crust
Then dump it beneath her loving breast

Chemical-ridden rain polluting all
We are destined for a global mighty fall
But no one cares, why should we anyway
Our lives are completely empty, yet, full of pollution at bay

Animals, birds and fish in the world sea
Are troubled by damage done by you and me
Trees dying, air, ozone, once starlit sky
Because of our thoughtlessness they will surely all die

Humans must see their great mistake!
Think of the world and all that is at stake!
Stop polluting, give Earth a break before it's too late!
Lost will be our patrimony, act now or permit senseless fate!

Alma Montgomery Frank

She Is Sick I Hear . . .

but fights on
despite a growing cancer in her veins.
Every shower chills her deep in acid rain
and I have a creeping fear:
Spring may not wake as usual next year.

But if it does it will be treated with the same presumption:
We will eat to satisfaction, and obesity,
and twirl at the carnival, crunching popcorn under our feet,
while back in the field they correct her dangerously:

Poison-spray her womb even to the vital seed,
irritate it to an obedient, chemotropic yield.
She is crawling scalded to meet her own Sahara
for the final death roll.

Scars from her persecution have already told:
Birds with guts on fire came with a thud.
The haul in the nets brought fish already dead.

She will not always heal, but one day
shrivel her breast to a crone's
and, stunned, abort her putrescent Eden
to a desert of skeletons.

Mary Alice

CRIMES AGAINST THE PLANET

People have lived on this planet and some have died!
Early deaths - but why the cause?
Can we blame the pollution in the air?
Or the vehicles on the roads, and the atomic rays?

The sun has been affected causing severe skin cancer
So researchers had found was it too much oxygen in the air?
Aircraft in the clouds may have been to blame!
All the seasons' weather now seems to merge -
A lot less fog, rain and snow, but what will happen in
the millennium - we shall not yet know!

God prophesied that the world would end up in fire -
Is it hell we are all going? It is not humans' desire -
We could all be destroyed, so Man has created his
own destiny -
Yes, Man had done it - affecting the balance of
our planet.

M E Smith

DAMAGE

They grew from a tiny seed
and their lives end with man's greed.
They are cut and chopped
then slashed and burned.
What will it take for the world to be turned.

How long can they keep this going
the brutal and savage mowing.
Gradually life is being destroyed.
We can't go on with continual taking
Never wondering about all the forsaking.

I wonder if they will ever stop
perhaps it is up to us to break the rot.
We have to learn to live in harmony
to look and see the damage being done
    to all the trees.

Alison Coveley

EARTH'S WARZONE

Amongst the rubble with the dead and dying,
An orphan child in hunger is crying.
While overhead bombs and bullets are flying,
And corpses unclaimed on the streets are lying.

Women and children lie suffering in bed,
They've lost a leg or maybe an arm.
A man is rushed in; blood pours from his head,
Just part of this cultural charm!

People suffering atrocity,
In a war created by men,
For what point the need of ferocity,
To kill again and again?

The point and purpose of the fight?
The rights to a stretch of land.
Is all sense of reason out of sight?
Why can't they just live hand in hand?

This Earth has space for us all to enjoy,
No matter where it may be.
No need to ruin, to kill and destroy,
Just for peace and for unity.

Tracy Howie

CIRCLE OF EXISTENCE

Each year the sun rotates the Earth,
Marking its boundary,
To the rest of the universe.
It's like how a panther,
Circles its prey,
Waiting for it to weaken,
Under its power.
Only the Earth weakens slower,
Than the prey.
This slow decay has its audience,
Venus, Mars, Jupiter and Pluto,
Watch while blue turns to black,
Life turns to death.
Monkeys, snakes, birds and beasts,
See the prey bring devoured.
Until the unwanted parts are left,
Left to rot into the ground they walk upon.
Every death has its audience,
But is it a far greater crime,
To stop the crime
Than the death.

Emily Havis (13)

TIME TO REFLECT

If the world revolves on an axis, one that will never break,
At least that's what we all hope, for a terrible mess it would make,
Land would roll over into the sea, the sea giant waterfalls make,
Mountains and trees would lean and fall to render an almighty quake.

Buildings would all lean sideways, turning things upside down,
Where's the sun and where's the moon and which way leads
out of town?
Out in the country there would be no fields just craters far and wide
Where have all the animals gone with many of us beside?

It's all too awful to contemplate, too late for us to think,
That we should have cared for our planet if we never wanted to sink,
Is this what we really want to leave for a future generation?
Something like this or worse could happen, lest we take evasive action.

We are being warned about global warming, toxic omissions and such
But we're not prepared to sacrifice the cars we love so much,
We do not own our planet, just custodians we be
So each and every one of us should protect it collectively.

Little but late will recompense, and us save from the consequence.

D Naylor

CRIMES AGAINST THE PLANET

What kind of world
is it we live in
Where countries are at
war all the time?
When we were young
we were taught to be good and kind,
also respect for each other.
Now that seems to be a crime.
Fifty years living here and seeing
the damage to the planet,
a crime we have done.
Chemical wars, and famine, drought. Why?
Because no one has really won.
If we go on in this way much longer,
exhausting our resources -
in the air, sea and under the ground,
poor Mother Earth won't have anything,
anymore to give . . .
. . . Then we'll understand
That will be the end of mankind.

Brian Mitchell

A Field's Worth

This place has a cricket team
  with players young and old.
Their matches have to be away,
  so problems come untold.
They have no field - not anywhere -
  it's built on or been sold.

Space there was in plenty - long
  before the cricket club -
Just a row of houses then,
  a church, a shop, a pub.
But now the land is built on, filled
  with houses, that's the rub.

There's one field at the middle school -
  redundant in its prime,
That's going to be a retail park.
  The team think it's a crime.
The council need the cash, they say,
  not trees for kids to climb.

The cricketers applied for space
  several miles away,
But this was turned down flat. It seems
  they're not allowed to play.
The problems they continue and
  the team lives day to day.

A cricket team without a field!
  For cash a field is sold!
The children of tomorrow, (if
  I may be so bold)
Will look at us with horror, when
  this true tale is told.

Marj Norton

Happy New Year

'Happy New Year, and cheers!' you say; I say to you;
while wondering silently, what will be new?
Merely a number
to help us mark the passing of today?
But after Hogmanay, what then?
Shall we just lumber on in the same old way,
follow the fretful crowd jostling for space
and take our place in the interminable queue
of hungry eyes that scan and scour,
and even when replete yearn to devour
some further impulse buying throw-away?
What labour-cheated bargains!
Products of those who toil
(no let-up, leave or leisure)
to fill our plastic bags,
doomed some sad day to add
their minim-measure more dioxin to the soil.
At last, the till; then street-tired, aching feet
weighed down by all the trash and treasure
beat a retreat.
Sweet home! A mini fort
secure with motte and moat;
the longed-for pot of tea;
slump into cushioned ease
and slumber. Reach for *The Sunday Times*;
focus those hopes for New Year Peace
and for a better world
upon some palm-fringed, unpolluted beach.

Then raise the glass again to wish each other cheer:
'Happy New Year!'

Wyn Cornish

A Recipe For Conservation

C ontrol the pillage of the seas,
now that would be a start.
O utlaw the use of pesticides,
a cry from my own heart.
N ever more dump nuclear waste
wantonly in our land.
S top raping ancient hedgerows,
small fields ancestors planned.
E radicate all toxic waste
to leave the rivers pure.
R eplace felled trees with broad-leafed kinds -
no spruce for money's lure.
V egetation must be managed,
not ruthlessly stripped out.
A ddress problems of pollution -
it's urgent without doubt.
T ransport needs to be much cleaner
so trains must bear the load
I nstead of lorries, cars and such
that choke each long grey road.
O zone is another worry
most scientists agree.
N ow it needs investigation
or soon it won't be free!
M uch birth control is needed too
for food is running low.
E arth is fast becoming sterile
much plundered to re-grow.
N ow we're on a precipice,
one step and we must fall
U nless we can find solutions
Goodbye to one and all.

Paddy Jupp

The Man In The Moon

The man in the moon
Is he still watching
Wonder what he makes of it all
It's all been done, nothing is new
The ozone might worry him
But then it should worry us
The moon, will just have to watch
As we head for our own destruction
We cut down the rainforests
As we make a mess of our air
Polluting the rivers and streams
And the seas are no better
What have we got to be proud of today
We should look after the world that we've got
Or the man in the moon will be all alone
With no one to watch.

Margaret Roe

. . . Heart-Shaped World . . .

What world do we live in? What time and space?
Who are these silly things called the human race?
Don't we know, this isn't for us?
We are making a nuisance and all the fuss.
You know, if we had a clue we'd be a threat,
But there is not a chance in that I'll bet.
I don't know how we don't care sometimes,
The world in some pain and always in some crimes.
We sit back and watch it fall,
I'll tell you something, we don't deserve this world at all!

Jamie Barnes

THE SPARKLING PAIN

They are drilling again
Sniffing the wine
Of the good Earth.
The sparkling pain
Of the diamond bit
Seeking the sweetmeat
Of long evolution.

They are boring once more
Enlarging a pore
Sucking the black crude
Yet not touching the core
For that burns like the cough
Of the volcanic heat
As nature signals her solution!

They are cutting the trees
Clearing the fields
Starving the fauna
Rare species now in a corner.
Destruction with ease
To house the well-heeled.
Burying the flora
Collapsing the caverns
Holding the wine
That feeds an industrial vein.
Celebrate in the taverns
The mechanical borer
Then see man decline
From the sparkling pain
Now in retreat
From his own revolution.

John Aldred

Welcome To Cardboard City!

'Welcome to Cardboard City',
The young man said to me,
'This corrugated edifice
Was once a splendid tree,
It stood out in the forest,
Majestic, straight and tall,
A refuge and a haven
For God's creatures, great and small.

Then a metamorphosis
Occurred in that old tree,
We owe its transformation
To our modern society,
It underwent a process,
Chopped down and pulped to paste,
Turned into cardboard cartons,
Oh what a shameful waste!

Now my home's disintegrating
and very soon will be,
No earthly use to man nor beast,
I'm sure you will agree,
That it would have been better
To have spared that splendid tree,
Absorbing all the toxins
To make air pollution free.

What a truly glorious place,
This planet Earth could be,
If man and nature learned to live
In perfect harmony!'

Nancy Gray

No Memories

All tomorrows have now gone,
Only memories linger on.

While some may have been happy,
With some joy left in our heart.
But afraid a lot that are sad.
Memories that will not depart!

All tomorrows have now gone,
Only memories linger on.

For those that live for the past,
Feel sad it's no longer there.
Still look for opportunities,
Hopefully of happiness to share.

But tomorrows have now gone,
Only memories linger on.

Nothing worth hanging on to,
No love ever came this way.
For some life is just empty,
Just an experience one can say!

All tomorrows have now gone,
No memories linger on . . .

Ann Beard

The Future Is Bleak

The monkeys, giraffes, spiders and snakes
The other creatures never known
So happy in their little lives
Until there was a groan

A groan so loud it deafened
It was men and their machine
Then at once all the creatures knew
These machines were very mean

Then along they came 'God save us all'
They uprooted all their homes
They squashed the burrows, took the trees
How many dead? No one knows

On and on these noises went
Until it was very late
To the animals it was very clear
Either move or meet their fate

So in this poem I'm expressing
The problems that we cause
How would *you* like it
If all those homes were yours?

Kayleigh Petherick (12)

THE FACTORY, OVER BEAUTY

A blossoming meadow in summer I was,
a place to laugh, to play and to sing,
and have all the fun in the world.
Small children having the time of their lives,
jumping into the piles of leaves in autumn,
and getting them all tangled up in their hair and inside their coats.
I bore snowmen in winter all over my body, like freckles,
and the trees that I wore were covered in a gleaming white
sheet of snow
that shone proudly in the cold winter sun.
In spring I was hidden under a mat of bluebells, daisies and dandelions,
like a long flowing beard of sweet scented beauty,
and bees and wasps flocked all over me in a thick striped camouflage.
Those were the days before the high-flying businessmen came.
They built all over me until I only existed as a waste disposal area.
I was turned into a natural rubbish tip and, instead of daisies, I had oil,
instead of bluebells I had rust, and in place of my dandelions
there was mould.
I now had noise, filth and thick, poisoned oil.
Instead of my gleeful children playing football and shouting out loud,
I now had to cope with a toxic ooze that was slowly taking
away my life.
No more happy days, they were gone and I was about to follow them.
The so-called businessmen had finally got what they wanted.
I now no longer existed, and the next generation had no field
for football, any more.
The sweet-scented summer meadow that had once thrived
with wildlife was gone.
All that was now left was a large hole filled with junk,
garbage and debris,
accompanied by a hugely misused, derelict factory that had
once been me.

Adam Jones (13)

By Hands Of Man

Stands Mother Nature, judge and jury,
Her judgement wrath, her justice fury,
For the rape of Earth, by hands of man,
Who choked her air, and ravaged her land.

Who robbed and plundered, her valuable stores,
Gorging, wasting and depriving her more,
These merely the tip of his iceberg of crime,
His tyranny more monstrous, with the passage of time.

Till his poisonous pollution, no walls confined,
Consuming, inhabiting, every cell and mind,
All contaminated via his tasks,
Faun and fauna, solid, liquid and gas.

Forcing production beyond his needs,
Spurred by zealous, fathomless greed,
Fertilizers and pesticides,
Subtracted as much as they multiplied.

Chemicals seeped though often ran,
Unseen, unhidden, throughout the land,
Leaking into river and lake,
Disturbing the balance of all in its wake.

The more man sprayed, the more was killed,
Over and under the earth he tilled,
Flowing ceaselessly into the sea,
Till a cesspool's what it came to be.

Its purity sapped by the spoils of strife,
Mutation, deformity, and radioactive life,
Past and present, man, woman and child,
For these passive or active crimes will be tried.

When the sentence falls, how will you plead?
Innocent or guilty of a single deed?

Sarah E Millar

SAD TIMES

What's happening to our world today
I think they're going mad
With all these guns, bombs and planes
I think it's very sad . . .

They're killing all these people
And little children too
They're knocking down their houses
With nowhere else to go . . .

They're destroying our environment
All wild life and the trees
With all this pollution
In rivers and the seas . . .

No decent clothes they have
They're mostly tattered and torn
And women with little children
With some who've just been born . . .

Why can't they work together
And try to put things right
Then put all the guns away
And then they would not fight . . .

B Salter

CRIME AGAINST NATURE

Nature, grand and unforgiving
Is starting to fight back
There should be great misgiving
As she now starts to attack

The Arctic's getting warmer
The ice cap breaks away
The water level's rising
In places far away

The ozone layer's thinning
More danger from the sun
We must urgently consider
What should now be done

There are less birds and insects
Rainforests disappear
Wild animals face extinction
And yet we show no fear

We must all now make a stand
There's things we can't replace
Have we really thought about
The future of our race?

Enid Gill

UNTITLED

The clouds so still and white
a cool summer's day
those images, these pictures
they're gone, years away
the clouds are black and grey
with all the pollution
we should be happy we live today
the grass is green
the sea is blue
of paint and dyes
lots of chemicals too
the fish are dead
the oil's gone
this existence we should dread
or we'll join the fish before long
the buildings are black
the ground dug up
humanity they lack
as the government says: shut up
we'll clean it up
say politicians
soon as you vote us in
then we can take bribes
to let them run amok
and destroy all our lives

Stafan Dunkelgrün

Saving The Planet

Our planet has suffered destruction over centuries of time
By man and his inventions, they've committed such a crime
Our factories and motor vehicles are causing much pollution
Damaging the ozone layer, we must act to find a solution

When going to the garage for petrol for the car
It's better to have unleaded than diesel or Four Star
Local authorities are doing their bit, so not to neglect
Recyclable household waste they now specially collect

We all tend to waste water, let it just run down the sink
When next washing our hands, we should stop and think
Such a precious commodity that could soon be in short supply
We all need water to wash and drink or else we will die

A water-butt could soon be every gardener's tool
Providing the summer water to keep the garden cool
Having a water meter fitted would help you think of the cost
Any water being wasted, is money that you have lost

We could all help the planet by saving energy at home
By insulating our lofts and filling walls with cavity foam
Draft excluder round windows and doors to keep homes draft-free
Switching off an unneeded light; turning heating down a degree

It is up to us all to save the planet, as time will not wait
This problem must be tackled now before it is too late
We must try to save the rainforests, stop pollution in the sky
Get the planet back to how it was, before its inhabitants all die

Linda Brown

Our Shameful Legacy

Mankind's stupidity has decimated planet Earth
And has failed to honour this world's true worth.
With CFC gases to create an ozone hole
Which have led to the thawing of the Arctic Pole.

Rainforests have been chopped and strewn,
This wanton folly cannot end too soon.
Add to this the slaughter of dolphin and whale,
Another sorrowful chapter in this atrocious tale.

Earth's oceans are polluted by toxic waste
Greed and avarice at alarming haste.
Poisoned rivers flow and meander to the sea
Where migrating salmon no longer swim free.

Fossil fuel gases encircle our globe,
Cloaking ozone and oxygen: a poisonous robe!
Toxic wastes, they maim and they kill,
Bending to humanity's thoughtless will.

Elephant and rhino: for ivory almost extinct
By an 'intelligent' species who hunt them to the brink.
Lions, tigers, other species recede by the score
When they are gone will it be forever more?

Mountain gorillas, apes, other primates too,
Slaughtered in natural environments, or confined in a zoo
The oceans are fished until they can sustain no more
Only dead and dying species will reach our shore.

As the new millennium approaches the human race
It is imperative that we show a more spiritual face.
The legacy of our young should be of hope and yearning
Not yet too late for compassion and learning.

Jim Wilson

ALIENS

Alien bushes, alien trees
Across our native land.
Alien viruses, alien germs,
All getting out of hand.
Alien shapes and alien shades
Flitting round our country glades.
Alien sounds and alien smells
Invade our mountain dells.

Alien flowers, alien crops,
Firmly taking root,
Alien fishes, alien birds,
Virgin territories dispute.
Alien flies and alien seeds,
Alien worms and alien weeds
Creating new hazards, creating new strife,
Defeating our native country life.

Alien frogs and alien snakes,
These will soon abound
And puma cats and coypu rats
Can now be seen around.
Grey squirrel, mink and kangaroo,
Marino sheep and fallow deer too,
All thriving and doing great,
While local lives deteriorate.

Chickens, rabbits, pheasants, turkeys
They all came from elsewhere,
Tomatoes and beans, potatoes and greens
These also are foreign fare.
Aliens, aliens, everywhere, not just in our native land,
Aliens, aliens, everywhere, too late, we understand.

R L Cooper

LIFE PULSE

The heat, the ice, the sun, the rain,
From furnace to glacier, or rock bound terrain
Storm-swept sea and calm, tranquil bay,
Tornado, zephyr soft mistral gently sway

Fluffing clouds, a hasty charade
Sweeping the treetops, peacock parade
Life in the rainforest quickens and paces
Animal stampede, hooves, senses races

Nature's impact always alert
Beating wings, magnificent, mute, broken, inert
Stalking, hiding, bending the grasses
Then leaping, wild survival, anything passes.

The scurrying ant, an eternal war
Protect their kingdom from enemies bar
In the air an insect cloud
their world too would overcrowd

Nature's hard lesson must it always be so,
Life not be simple, more caring, more slow,
As tender gorilla nurturing her young
Brown-eyed glow from her heart songs unsung

Is man then the most base of all
Not only for survival, his cruelty fall
Ignorance perhaps, a belated plea
Lash-hooded eyes, he cannot see.

Widen then those tight closed lids
Look further afield, as your instinct bids,
Swiftly now, be vigilant and learn
Laggard too long, our planet burn.

Grace Wade

POLLUTION'S SOLUTIONS

The ozone layer haunts us all -
A truly tragic wake-up call!
Each year it weakens more and more -
Something the wise will not ignore!
The damage stands the test of time -
Thus proving mighty is the crime
That causes cancers to the skin
And brings to home Man's awful sin!
This world that we call planet Earth
Is creamed of everything of worth
The gold and silver, oil, too,
Once precious gifts yet now they're few!
Alack, alas! Let's wring our hands!
Like Alice locked in wonderlands!
Midst fantasies we couldn't tell
Our planet's doomed, destined for hell!
We're trapped unless we all repent.
And learn to be the planet's friend!
'Too late!' some cry . . . 'Too late to change!'
Is it too late to rearrange?
God helps the ones who help themselves -
Let's not leave troubles on the shelves!
Let's all clean house! What can we find?
Clean up your act and save Mankind!
If not, then suffer like the rest
Who spurn advice and won't be blessed!
'Pollution's solutions?' They're up to you . . .
God bless the good things that you do . . .

Denis Martindale

Religion

Global talons claw at reason,
Scratching through such unseeing eyes.
To minds askew with mental treason,
Falling angels, `brimming with lies.

From books the words precipitate
Obsessive cries of sinless gain,
In mosque and church they congregate,
Idolatrous frenzies breeding disdain.

Tomes of scripture feed on frailty
As objective thought goes down the pan,
Each page the voice of deity!
When every sentence comes from man . . .!

Offspring drugged from birth with tosh
Are left devoid of choice and sense,
Inbred, fed with traditional nosh
'Til bloated, stuffed with arrogance.

Once matured and fat with praise,
Conducted by batons laced in pride,
They waltz to Jihad and Crusade
Then piously mourn those who died

Essem Teigh

Our Shame!

Thought destroyed my appetite today.
The food I had taken in my gullet stuck.
Thoughts of a child, bloated, starving - lay,
Awaiting the arrival of food-laden truck.

More must be done to solve this blight.
The disgrace we all share, must be faced.
Our greed and apathy cannot be right,
Life without charity, has hate interlaced.

Their future is ours, we really must see.
Our lives are comforted with plentiful breast.
It has never intended, all riches should be
Ours, at the expense of a shrunken rest.

Wars, pestilence, famine and hatred
To the dying child, they are one and the same.
What are the reasons? We hear berated.
Not our fault, don't try us to blame!

What can we do? Is often the cry.
We must together force the world's hand,
To find a solution, the aim must be high.
To join us all in a compassionate band . . .

Maurice Wilkinson

POLLUTION

Pollution is spreading
The sky ain't so blue.
Look into the future
What can we do!

The world it is changing
Around us each day.
Looks like pollution
Might be here to stay!

Self preservations
A natural thing.
But while there's pollution
It don't mean a thing!

You're smoking, you're choking
You're killing yourselves.
So pack up your fags
Lets drink to good health!

Perhaps when we're older
And wiser, maybe!
We'll look to the past
And then we will see!

Pollution is spreading
The sea ain't so blue.
Look into the future
What can we do!

K D Thomas

MUCOUS MEMBRANE

Stepping over skin of seaweed
Stretched scar-tissue taut
Fine diaphanous membrane
Clinging to life supporting rocks.

Reflected like silk webs
Spun in bright sunshine
Along serrated edge of a thin tide
Leaving visible as it ebbs
The still quivering, amorphic mass of
New corpses. Another day's pass.

Fusion of plankton, crustaceans' shells
Laid bare on the naked shore
Dying colours of a dying landscape
Glimpsed as we pass on the incoming tide.

No life visible on jagged outcrops
Of rocks thrown there by volcanic upheavals
Anchored by barnacles, littered with
Skeletal remains, now metamorphic props,
Perches for lone cormorants hanging out to dry
Scanning a watery sun under a winter sky.

A barren place now, where souls lie undisturbed,
Forsaken, waterless graveyard
Where, raked underfoot,
They were left to die . . .

Heather Bruyère Watt